to

_____

from

_____

date

_____

Bring

— ON THE —

Merry

25 DAYS OF GREAT JOY
FOR CHRISTMAS

CANDACE CAMERON BURE

DaySpring
LIVE YOUR FAITH

Bring On The Merry: 25 Days of Great Joy for Christmas
Copyright © 2021 by Candace Cameron Bure. Used under license Candaché, Inc., all rights reserved.
First Edition, July 2021

Published by:

DaySpring

21154 Highway 16 East
Siloam Springs, AR 72761
dayspring.com

Produced with the assistance of Peachtree Publishing Services.
Cover Design by: Jessica Wei

Printed in China
Prime: J4970
ISBN: 978-1-64454-989-6

It's the Christmas season, friends! I truly think it is the most wonderful time of the year. It's a season of all my favorite things: family, Hallmark Christmas movies, gift giving, and, of course, time with the One who gives us a reason to celebrate: Jesus. Throughout the next twenty-five days, I hope your joy grows exponentially. I hope you experience the merriment of Christmastime like never before. I pray that you will find true rest and peace and purpose during this crazy season.

In *Bring On the Merry*, you will find daily devotionals that point you to life-changing words from the Bible and encourage you to focus on living in a relationship with Jesus—especially during this busy time of the year. You'll also have the opportunity to work through interactive activities designed to guide you in reflecting more deeply on what you have read. In addition, you'll read classic Christmas stories, poems, and song lyrics to help you celebrate the season. My desire is that this book will illuminate the beauty of Christmas in a fresh way. I can't wait for you to dive in. I hope this will be your most merry Christmas yet!

SCAN FOR
MORE MERRY
FROM CANDACE!

Candace

Ready to Serve

I've always wondered what it was like to be Mary. A young woman, unmarried, not ready to have babies (is anyone really ever *ready*?), not ready to carry the responsibility and burden of giving up her body, her time, and her life for the sake of another. But when the angel visits her and tells her of her weighty task, she responds: "Yes, I see it all now: I'm the Lord's maid, ready to serve" (LUKE 1:38 THE MESSAGE).

It's hard to imagine responding with that level of willingness and confidence in God's good plan. Around the holidays, we often get swept up in our own expectations, hopes, and dreams. We want our holiday parties to feel effortless—beautifully presented food, natural conversation, a white elephant exchange that balances fun with a healthy hint of competition. We scour stores for the perfect gifts that will make our loved ones feel seen and appreciated. We stay up all night wrapping gifts, nibbling on cookies, and drinking hot chocolate by the fire. Our hopes and expectations surrounding the holidays are not all bad—in fact, they often circle around making others happy. But at the end of the day, what if we are missing the true joy of Christmas?

When Mary heard from the angel on that fateful day, the purpose of Christ's coming was clear: Mary had a vision of service and a life marked by sacrifice. She gave herself to this life and painted a beautiful picture for women today to follow after.

It's most important to notice that while Mary's response seems almost supernatural, what she did was extremely natural. She carried and gave birth to a child. It's something that billions of women have done. It's so important for us to notice this because it points to what is actually important. It's not the magnitude of what she does—a great achievement or a skill that surpasses everyone else. She doesn't out-host or out-speak or out-gift anyone else. Her life is not marked by incredible accomplishment or clout. She is honored because of her obedience and willingness to say *yes*. Mary models a heart that is willing to serve and give her everything to a God who loves her.

The beauty of Mary's life is that we have access to that same incredible joy. In the midst of this crazy holiday season, what do you sense God nudging you to say yes to? Where do you feel a gentle tug to respond, "I'm ready to serve"? Maybe you're thinking about partnering with an organization like the Salvation Army or Compassion International—two fantastic nonprofits that my family supports—to help meet needs of people around the world. Or maybe there's someone in your neighborhood who is in need. Are there opportunities in your town to volunteer to serve people who are sick, lonely, or hurting? Or maybe there's someone within your own family who is hurting this season. Is there someone who needs an extra dose of care or service this Christmas? Maybe your spouse is in desperate need of encouragement or your child is in need of an afternoon alone with Mom.

However you feel God tugging on your heart, know that a life of simple service is a life that is honored by God. After the angel visits Mary, she tells her cousin Elizabeth about the encounter. Elizabeth responds enthusiastically with "Blessed are you among women!" (LUKE 1:42 NKJV). That is the beauty of giving up your own expectations and hopes for the simple steps of obedience laid out by Jesus. Blessing! Joy! Fulfillment! This Christmas, keep your eyes open for moments where you, too, might willingly respond, "I see it all now: I'm . . . ready to serve."

The Legend of the Christmas Tree

by Lucy Wheelock

Two little children were sitting by the fire one cold winter's night. All at once they heard a timid knock at the door, and one ran to open it. There, outside in the cold and the darkness, stood a child with no shoes upon his feet and clad in thin, ragged garments. He was shivering with cold, and he asked to come in and warm himself.

"Yes, come," cried both the children. "You shall have our place by the fire. Come in!"

They drew the little stranger to their warm seat and shared their supper with him and gave him their bed, while they slept on a hard bench. In the night they were awakened by strains of sweet music and, looking out, they saw a band of children in shining garments approaching the house. They were playing on golden harps, and the air was full of melody.

Suddenly the Stranger Child stood before them, no longer cold and ragged but clad in silvery light. His soft voice said, "I was cold, and you took Me in. I was hungry, and you fed Me. I was tired, and you gave Me your bed. I am the Christ Child, wandering through the world to bring peace and happiness to all good children. As you have given to Me, so may this tree every year give rich fruit to you."

So saying, He broke a branch from the fir tree that grew near the door, and He planted it in the ground and disappeared. But the branch grew into a great tree, and every year it bore wonderful golden fruit for the kind children.

What gets in the way of you being ready to serve?
(Check all that apply.)

- [ ] Lack of direction
- [ ] Fear
- [x] Busyness
- [ ] Waiting for the perfect conditions
- [ ] Thinking you have nothing to offer
- [ ] Other: _____

What are ways that you naturally love to serve? List them below.

Example: donate products, feed the hungry, mentor...

donate, work with youth,
organizational work

Where do you see needs in your current community?

COLOR IN THE ICONS

School

Animal shelter

Homeless shelter

Food pantry

Youth services

Senior Home

Where else can you serve? Draw those places here.

How can you make time and space to say "I'm ready to serve" to God this Christmas season? *Fill out the time management graph below and add in a few hours this week to serve.*

EXAMPLE

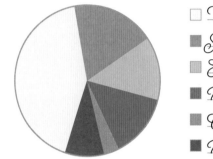

☐ *Work* _____

◼ *Sleep* _____

◻ *Eating/Cooking* _____

◼ *Playing/Entertainment* _____

◼ *Cleaning* _____

◼ *Reading* _____

YOUR TURN

KEY

☐ _____

☐ _____

☐ _____

☐ _____

☐ _____

☐ _____

☐ _____

Joy to the world! the Lord is come;
Let earth receive her King;
Let every heart prepare Him room,
And heaven and nature sing,
And heaven and nature sing,
And heaven, and heaven, and nature sing....
He rules the world with truth and grace,
And makes the nations prove
The glories of His righteousness,
And wonders of His love,
And wonders of His love,
And wonders, wonders, of His love

—FROM "JOY TO THE WORLD"
BY ISAAC WATTS

Giving Thanks

I know Thanksgiving is *so* last month, but the beauty of giving thanks is that its power is available at any time of the year. During this season, we have so much to be thankful for.

Sometimes I'm so focused on my to-do list that I forget to be still, to stop and appreciate all the beauty around me. Why is it so *hard* to be still? Can you relate? I've found that being intentional about stopping and thanking God for what He's given me is incredibly powerful. Having a bad morning? Find something to be thankful for. Overwhelmed by your to-do lists? Find something to be thankful for. Gratitude doesn't change your circumstances, but it does awaken your heart to the full reality of your situation. So often it's easy for us to be focused on a small part of what's really going on. This small part can leave me feeling discouraged, overwhelmed, or discontent. But when I zoom out and look for what is great about my life and situation, I am never left wanting.

In Psalm 107 the psalmist writes, "Give thanks to the Lord, for He is good; His love endures forever. Let the redeemed of the Lord tell their story—those He redeemed from the hand of the foe, those He gathered from the lands, from east and west, from north and south" (VERSES 1-3 NIV). Although we don't often use words like "hand of the foe," we can imagine what this means for us today. Have you experienced the love of God? Then you have a story to tell! Think about obstacles in your own life. Consider what opposes you.

Those obstacles and oppositions are your enemy, your foe, and God has redeemed you from them. Give thanks to God for the way He has redeemed your life. For the beauty He has made from ashes.

The psalmist goes on to celebrate that God "gathered from the lands." I love this image. It makes me think of God gathering up His children, one by one, and bringing them to a place of safety and respite. How has God rescued you? Maybe from a physical situation, an illness, or a sinful pattern? Give thanks to God for this rescue!

Let your gratitude change the way you view the world and other people. Walk through your day today and give thanks for the opportunities God provides you with. Maybe it's the chance to notice something you're thankful for in your child. Thank God for this! Maybe you need to stop when you leave your house and enjoy the beautiful breeze on your face or the feeling of a snowflake on your cheek. Stop and give thanks to God for the ability to experience His beautiful creation. Look around at the good gifts He has given you and follow in the psalmist's example: "Give thanks to the LORD."

The psalmist goes on to encourage us further: "Let them give thanks to the LORD for His unfailing love and His wonderful deeds for mankind, for He satisfies the thirsty and fills the hungry with good things" (PSALM 107:8-9 NIV). What comes to your mind when you think of being filled with good things? How has God filled you up during this Christmas season? Perhaps it's not with physical nourishment but spiritual food. Maybe it's a new podcast you stumbled across or a friendship that is providing encouragement and joy.

Whatever your circumstances, take time today to thank God for His unfailing love! This is a love that gives without expectation or limit; it's a love that provides satisfying life, a love that gives good gifts, and a love that transforms brokenness. I am blown away by this love! Do as the psalmist did and tell your story of God's good and redeeming work in your life.

Tiny Tim

by Charles Dickens (ADAPTED)

There was once a man who did not like Christmas. His name was Scrooge, and he was a hard, sour-tempered man of business, intent only on saving and making money and caring nothing for anyone. He paid the poor, hardworking clerk in his office, Bob Cratchit, as little as he could and lived on as little as possible himself, alone, in two dismal rooms. He was never merry, comfortable, or happy, and he hated other people to be so. That's why he hated Christmas.

On Christmas Eve, Mr. Scrooge, having reluctantly given his poor clerk permission to spend Christmas Day at home, locked up his office and went home in a very bad temper. After he got into bed, he had some wonderful and disagreeable dreams.

Bob Cratchit had a wife and five other children besides Tiny Tim, who was a weak, delicate little cripple, gentle, patient, and loving, with a sweet face. Mr. Cratchit carried his little boy on his shoulder to see the shops and people, and today he had taken him to church for the first time.

When Mr. Cratchit came home, his long comforter hanging three feet under his threadbare coat because he had no topcoat, Tiny Tim was perched on his shoulder.

"And how did Tim behave?" asked Mrs. Cratchit.

"As good as gold and better," replied his father. "He told me that he hoped the people in church, who saw he was a cripple, would remember on

Christmas Day who it was who made the lame to walk."

Mrs. Cratchit proudly placed a goose upon the table. After the family ate, they gathered around the fire. Mr. Cratchit served round some hot sweet stuff out of a jug and said, "A merry Christmas to us all, my dears, God bless us."

"God bless us, every one," echoed Tim, and then they drank to each other's health, and Mr. Scrooge's health, and told stories and sang songs.

In one of Mr. Scrooge's dreams on Christmas Eve, a Christmas spirit showed him his clerk's home; he saw them all, heard them drink to his health, and took special note of Tiny Tim.

On Christmas night he had more dreams, and the spirit took him again to his clerk's poor home.

Upstairs, the father, with his face hidden in his hands, sat beside a little bed, on which lay a tiny figure, white and still. "Tiny Tim died because his father was too poor to give him what was necessary to make him well; you kept him poor," said the dream-spirit to Mr. Scrooge.

Mr. Scrooge saw all this and woke the next morning feeling as he had never felt in his life. "I'm as light as a feather, and as happy as an angel, and as merry as a schoolboy," he said to himself. "I hope everybody had a merry Christmas, and here's a happy New Year to all the world."

Poor Bob Cratchit crept into the office a few minutes late, expecting to be scolded for it, but Mr. Scrooge smiled as he shook hands with his clerk, telling him he was going to raise his salary and asking affectionately after Tiny Tim! "Make up a good fire in your room before you set to work, Bob," he said as he closed the door.

Bob could hardly believe his eyes and ears! Mr. Scrooge sent them a turkey for dinner, and Tiny Tim had his share, for Tiny Tim did not die. Mr. Scrooge became a second father to him; he wanted for nothing, and grew up strong and hearty. Mr. Scrooge loved him because Tiny Tim had unconsciously, through the Christmas dream-spirit, touched his hard heart and caused him to become a good and happy man.

Keep thanksgiving a real part of the Christmas season. Read the following verses in this psalm of thanksgiving. As you read the verses below, trace the words on the right side of the page as you think through all the things you are thankful for this season. Think of the gifts in your life that are big and small. Fill these pages with the many good gifts God has given you.

I will always thank the LORD;
  I will never stop praising Him.
I will praise Him for what He has done;
  may all who are oppressed listen and be glad!
Proclaim with me the LORD's greatness;
  let us praise His name together!
I prayed to the LORD, and He answered me;
  He freed me from all my fears.
The oppressed look to Him and are glad;
  they will never be disappointed.
The helpless call to Him, and He answers;
  He saves them from all their troubles.
His angel guards those who honor the LORD
  and rescues them from danger.
Find out for yourself how good the LORD is.
  Happy are those who find safety with Him.
Honor the LORD, all His people;
  those who obey Him have all they need.
Even lions go hungry for lack of food,
  but those who obey the LORD lack nothing good.

PSALM 34:1–10 (GNT)

Thank
the Lord

Praise
Him

He
freed
me

He
answers

Happy
are those
who find safety
in Him

Thinking through why we are thankful for the people in our lives can help us when it comes to choosing the right gifts for our family and loved ones. Take time to fill in the chart below and you're sure to have the winning gifts for all those in your life this year.

GIFT RECIPIENT	WHY I AM THANKFUL FOR THEM	WHAT GIFT WILL SHOW MY GRATITUDE

The shepherds had an angel,
The wise men had a star;
But what have I, a little child,
To guide me home from far,
Where glad stars sing together,
And singing angels are?
Lord Jesus is my Guardian,
So I can nothing lack . . .
Lord, bring me nearer day by day,
Till I my voice unite,
And sing my Glory, glory,
With angels clad in white.
All Glory, glory, giv'n to Thee,
Thro' all the heav'nly height.

—FROM "THE SHEPHERDS HAD AN ANGEL"
BY CHRISTINA G. ROSSETTI

It Takes a Village

People shine in different ways around Christmastime. I'm a Christmas card girl myself. I love sending out a fun and beautiful card that captures the joy of the holiday with my family. Maybe you're creative in the way you decorate your Christmas tree or you make *really* good sugar cookies. Maybe you've got a knack for picking super thoughtful gifts for the people you love. Everyone has something to bring to the table. My favorite way to throw a Christmas party is to ask every guest to bring something that brings them joy. One friend brings the appetizer, another helps me decorate before the party, another brings beautiful flowers to make the space more festive. It should be a season to celebrate the ways we bring joy to each other and use the gifts God's given us.

It reminds me of Jesus' birth in a way. Everyone had a role to play; everyone contributed to the story, but still at the center of it all was Jesus. His birth ultimately gave meaning and purpose to the profound role Mary played in carrying Him in her body for nine months. The shepherds' presence in the field, doing what they were made to do, allowed them to see the angel and become messengers of Jesus' arrival. Even the donkey, created by God, did holy work carrying Jesus' mother to the inn that day. Christmas is a time to celebrate the meaning and purpose that Christ's birth gives our everyday lives.

A simple Christmas card can provide encouragement to someone who is going through a hard time—filling their home with smiling faces and reminders of how much they matter. A plate of Christmas cookies might be just what the mother of three kids under three needs to find that quiet five minutes she's been desperate for.

Christmas is a season of joy! And what greater joy is there than using the gifts God has given you to bless others and celebrate the birth of Jesus? First Corinthians 12:26-27 remind us that "if one part is honored, every part rejoices with it. Now you are the body of Christ, and each one of you is a part of it" (NIV). We are created to live and enjoy life within a group of people who are different from us and help us experience the kingdom of God in new and beautiful ways.

This Christmas, think about how God made you. What about *you* brings God and others so much joy? Is it your famous Christmas dinner? Your warm hospitality that makes people feel at home? Or the gift that shows you really care? Or maybe it's something less tangible. Is it a knowing hug for a friend who's hurting this Christmas season or the compassionate words in a card to a friend who's lost a loved one? Is it your love for serving those who have less than you in a time that is focused on attaining more? Maybe it's providing a verse of encouragement or a listening ear to someone dreading another difficult Christmas dinner with her family.

God gifts each of us in different ways, but each gift makes this season rich and full of joy. Spend time this year thinking about how you can bring joy to others through your unique gifts. Relish the fact that God made you specifically to bless the world in a way only you can, whether it's through words, actions, prayer, or service. Be confident in your ability to spread the love of Jesus in your own unique and beautiful way.

Why the Chimes Rang

by Raymond McAlden

There was once in a faraway country a wonderful church that stood on a high hill in the midst of a great city. And every Sunday, as well as on sacred days like Christmas, thousands of people climbed the hill to its great archways. At one corner of the church was a great gray tower, and at the top of the tower was a chime of Christmas bells. They had hung there ever since the church had been built and were the most beautiful bells in the world.

It was the custom on Christmas Eve for all the people to bring to the church their offerings to the Christ Child, and when the best offering was laid on the altar, there used to come sounding through the music of the choir the Christmas chimes far up in the tower. But for many long years they had never been heard. Every Christmas Eve the rich people still crowded to the altar, each one trying to bring some better gift than any other. But although the service was splendid and the offerings plenty, only the roar of the wind could be heard far up in the stone tower.

A number of miles from the city lived a boy named Pedro and his little brother. They knew very little about the Christmas chimes, but they had heard of the service in the church on Christmas Eve and had a secret plan to go to see the beautiful celebration.

The day before Christmas was bitterly cold. Pedro and Little Brother slipped quietly away early in the afternoon. Before nightfall they had trudged so far, hand in hand, that they saw the lights of the big city just ahead of them. They were about to enter one of the gates when they saw something dark on the snow near their path. It was a poor woman who had fallen just outside the city, too sick and tired to move on. Pedro knelt down beside her and tried to rouse her, even tugging at her arm a little.

"It's no use, Little Brother," said Pedro. "You will have to go on alone. This woman will freeze to death if nobody cares for her. When you come back you can bring someone to help her. I will keep her from freezing and perhaps get her to eat the bun that is left in my pocket. You can easily find your way to church, and you must see and hear everything twice—once for you and once for me. I am sure the Christ Child must know how I should love to come with you and worship Him. And oh! If you get a chance, take this little silver piece of mine and lay it down for my offering when no one is looking." In this way he hurried Little Brother off to the city and winked hard to keep back the tears.

The great church was a wonderful place that night. At the close of the service came the procession with the offerings to be laid on the altar. Rich men marched proudly up to offer their gifts of jewels and gold to the Christ Child. And last of all walked the king, who took from his head the royal crown, all set with precious stones, and laid it gleaming on the altar. "Surely," everyone said, "we shall hear the bells now, for nothing like this has ever happened before." But still only the cold wind was heard in the tower.

The choir began the closing hymn. Suddenly the organist stopped playing; the old minister was holding up his hand for silence. As the people strained their ears to listen, there came softly the sound of the chimes in the tower. So much sweeter were the notes than anything that had been heard before. Then all the people stared straight at the altar to see what great gift had awakened the long silent bells.

But all that the nearest of them saw was the childish figure of Little Brother, who had crept softly down the aisle when no one was looking and had laid Pedro's little piece of silver on the altar.

Take this time to think about the group of people you are surrounded by and how you can learn from and benefit from the wonderful ways God has gifted them.

Fill in the blanks with names and attributes of your friends and family members. Next to each name, write that person's unique gifts and how you appreciate and personally benefit from those gifts.

Example: __Kristy__ is so good at __making a cozy house__ for people to rest in. It gives me __space to be calm__ and __get away from the craziness__ .

I love _____ because he/she *(circle one)* is

so good at _____ and

it makes me feel _____ .

_____ always amazes me. He/she *(circle one)* is

really wonderful when it comes to _____ and

I'm so grateful God gave them the gift of _____ .

_____ is so much fun to be with!

He/She makes me laugh every time they _____ .

Now spend a few minutes celebrating the way *you* contribute to the body of Christ! Brainstorm your own gifts and how they translate into the Christmas season. Think through even the most practical ways God has gifted you and how you might use your gifts to spread joy to others this season.

Example: I love to _celebrate other people_ *through words! During Christmas I want to* _drop notes off_ *for* _friends_ *to encourage them and let them know* _how thankful I am for their friendship_ .

I have fun when I _____.

This Christmas, I'm going to take time to do just this!

And, I'll invite _____ to do it

with me so we can have fun together and create new memories.

God has given me the gift of _____.

This holiday season, I'm going to use this gift to encourage others

by _____.

God is so good! He showed me kindness when I _____

_____. Because of this, I want to show kindness.

This Christmas season, I'm going to do just that!

I'm going to _____ .

Living with Anticipation

Christmas is such an incredible time of anticipation. Your efforts and planning and preparing finally come together to pull off a (hopefully) wonderful and meaningful time with your family. One of my favorite parts of the Christmas season is imagining my kids' reactions when they open gifts. As they've gotten older, we've moved away from giving lots of smaller items and instead try to pick one bigger but really special gift. I love spending time thinking about what each of my kids would love to receive. As Christmas Day inches closer, my excitement surrounding gift giving grows! No matter how hard I plan or how thoughtful I might be, though, there is always a little seed of doubt in my head wondering if they will love their gifts.

So many years ago, the prophets foretold Jesus' birth. Isaiah wrote that He would "be called Wonderful Counselor, Mighty God, Everlasting Father, Prince of Peace" (ISAIAH 9:6 NLT). Can you imagine anticipating the arrival of a king like that? Despite knowing a good king was coming to Israel, the Israelites still wondered and wanted more. They still met difficult circumstances and disappointing outcomes. I have to imagine there was a small voice in their heads wondering if it could be as good as it seemed. Don't we all encounter moments where we hope and anticipate, only to hear the small voice of doubt creeping in?

All of us live in expectation and anticipation. We consider what will come next and how we will live in light of what's coming. I wonder what anticipation you are living with right now. What are you planning and hoping for? Are you anxiously awaiting the arrival of a new baby? Are you looking forward to reconnecting with an old friend? Is the wedding of your son or daughter right around the corner? Are you living for the next vacation or reunion or break from work? Each of these events, and countless more, are so worth anticipating. They are joyful moments that God orchestrates for us, but in the end even the moments we look forward to most are not enough to satisfy us.

Christmastime is a season of waiting and anticipating. Many stores start reminding us of the Christmas season in September with the arrival of decorations. We save for Christmas outings, pose for Christmas card photos, hunt for the perfect gifts, and dream about sitting under the tree on Christmas morning. But what we often realize after the dust settles on those Christmas mornings is that all the bustle and chaos of the season doesn't necessarily give us what we need. It doesn't satisfy the deepest longings of our souls.

No matter what you are expecting this Christmas season, there is one thing that we can expect and count on without a hint of doubt. We can expect to be met and cared for by a loving God! A God who fulfills His promises and continues to show up despite our doubts and questioning. Just thinking about that makes me smile. How about you? I'm sure there are lots of things you are excited about this Christmas. I know there will be plenty of beautiful, joyful moments with family and friends. But at the end of it all, remember that there is only one thing that will truly satisfy, and that is Jesus! Be encouraged by this. Let it bring you freedom and lightheartedness and confidence in God's plan unfolding in a way that is perfect and redemptive.

A Turkey for One

by *Lavinia S. Goodwin*

Lura's uncle Roy is in Japan. He used to have Christmas dinner at Lura's home. Now he could only write her papa to say a box of gifts had been sent, and one was for his little girl.

The little girl clapped her hands, crying, "Oh, Mamma! Don't you think it is the chain and locket dear uncle said he would sometime give me?"

"No," replied her papa, reading on. "Your uncle says it is a turkey for one."

"But we do not need turkeys from Japan," the little daughter remarked soberly.

Her papa smiled and handed the open letter to her mamma.

"Read it aloud, every bit," begged Lura, seeing her mamma was smiling too. But her mamma folded the letter and said nothing.

On Christmas Eve the box, which had just arrived, was opened, and everyone in the house was made glad with a present. Lura's was a papier-mâché turkey, nearly as large as the one brought home at the same time by the market boy.

The next morning, while the fowl in the kitchen was being roasted, Lura placed hers before a window and watched people admire it as they passed by. All its imitation feathers, and even more its red wattles, seemed to wish every man and woman, boy and girl, a merry Christmas.

Lura had not spoken of the jewelry since her uncle's letter was read. It is not nice for one who receives a gift to wish it were different. Lura was not that kind of child.

When dinner was nearly over, her papa said to her, "My dear, you have had as much of my turkey as you wanted. If you please, I will now try some of yours."

"Mine is what Uncle Roy calls a turkey for one," laughed Lura. She turned in her chair toward where her bird had been strutting on the windowsill and added with surprise, "Why, what has become of him?"

At that moment the servant brought in a huge platter. When room had been made for it on the table, it was set down in front of Lura's papa, and on the dish was her turkey.

"Oh, what fun!" the child exclaimed cheerfully. "Did Uncle tell you to pretend to serve it?"

"I have not yet finished what he directed me to do," her papa said, with a flourish of the carving knife.

"But, Papa—oh, please!" Lura pleaded. Her hand was on his arm. "You would not spoil my beautiful bird from Japan!"

Papa touched a hidden spring with the point of the knife. The breast opened and disclosed the fowl filled with choice toys and other things. The first taken out was a tiny box. Inside was a gold chain and locket; the locket held Uncle Roy's picture.

It was a turkey for one—for only Uncle Roy's niece. But all the family shared the amusement.

Oftentimes, unmet expectations come from not saying them out loud. Today, in the midst of a busy Christmas season, use this space to write down expectations you might be carrying with you toward God. Write a prayer explaining to Him your heart, your desires, your hopes, and even your fears.

MY EXPECTATIONS	KEY SCRIPTURES (REMIND ME WHERE MY CONTENTMENT COMES FROM)

My Prayer
FOR THIS HOLIDAY SEASON

_____
_____
_____

Answered Prayer
(COME BACK AND FILL THIS IN LATER)

_____
_____
_____

List all the ways
GOD HAS COME THROUGH FOR YOU
IN THE PAST—AND WHY YOU THINK
HE WILL DO IT AGAIN.

_____
_____
_____

The Waiting Game

Have you ever bought or received a chocolate Advent calendar, that ever-present reminder that Christmas is coming? Each morning you're met with a small token of Christmastime and with a reminder that Christmas is one day closer. Advent calendars are just one of the many ways we anticipate Christmas Day. Waiting during the holidays is just part of the season. We wait in long lines at department stores to purchase the perfect gift. We wait on our mail every day to look through beautiful Christmas cards. We wait for loved ones to return home to celebrate the holiday together. Waiting at Christmastime can feel never-ending, but it is so often worth the wait, isn't it?

Sometimes when we wait for things, though, it seems like the wait will not be worth it. I know I struggle with patience. Do you? Maybe you're waiting for a positive pregnancy test or a more optimistic test result. Maybe you're waiting to make things right with your spouse or for a job interview. Perhaps you're waiting for God to make Himself more real to you or for someone you love to recognize their need for Jesus.

Many times we grow weary during the waiting. We grow tired of mustering the hope to wait more, and we end up exhausted. The prophet Isaiah spoke to this feeling when he wrote: "Even youths shall faint and be weary, and young men shall fall exhausted; but they who wait for the LORD shall renew their strength; they shall mount up with wings like eagles; they shall run and not be weary; they shall walk and not faint" (ISAIAH 40:30–31 ESV).

Waiting and anticipating can leave us many places. Sometimes it leaves us eager and excited for what's next, but sometimes in the midst of our waiting we grow tired. We run out of steam and can't find the strength to carry on. In these moments, remember the words of Isaiah. Know that you are not alone in weariness. There are people all around you who have also grown tired. And in those moments when we are tired, God wants us to lean on Him.

I love the image of being renewed and mounting up on wings like eagles. Can you imagine the weightlessness and freedom you would feel soaring through the air? The burdens of the world would feel so far away. The beauty of waiting on God is that we can find that sort of freedom in this moment. We can look to the character of God and His ability to wait and release our tiredness to Him. It's hard to imagine the patience and steadfastness God possesses. How many times have we let Him down? How many times have we made promises that we haven't kept? How many times have we disobeyed, disregarded, and dismissed Him? And yet, God is a God of hope. He is a God who stays with us and will not let us go.

We have access to this sort of strength and endurance if we only lean on God! Are you tired? I know I often am! Do you feel like you don't have enough to keep going? Are you at the end of your rope and unsure if you want to keep waiting? Wait on the Lord! Let His consistency, His promises, His love carry you through this season of waiting. Be renewed by the strength of God's love for you. And don't forget to enjoy some Advent calendar chocolates while you wait.

The Christmas Babe

by Margaret E. Sangster

We love to think of Bethlehem,
  That little mountain town,
To which, on earth's first Christmas Day,
  Our blessed Lord came down.
A lowly manger for His bed,
  The cattle near in stall,
There, cradled close in Mary's arms,
  He slept, the Lord of all.

If we had been in Bethlehem,
  We too had hasted fain
To see the Babe whose little face
  Knew neither care nor pain.
Like any little child of ours,
  He came unto His own,
Through Cross and shame before Him stretched—
  His pathway to His Throne.

If we had dwelt in Bethlehem,
  We would have followed fast,
And where the Star had led our feet
  Have knelt ere dawn was past.
Our gifts, our songs, our prayers had been
  An offering, as He lay,
The blessed Babe of Bethlehem,
  In Mary's arms that day.

Now breaks the latest Christmas Morn!
  Again the angels sing,
And far and near the children throng
  Their happy hymns to bring.
All heaven is stirred! All earth is glad!
  For down the shining way,
The Lord who came to Bethlehem,
  Comes yet, on Christmas Day.

DEAR GOD,
HERE ARE FIVE
THINGS I'M
WAITING ON

IF I'M HONEST,
THIS IS HOW MUCH
I'M TRUSTING YOU
WITH IT

FULLY   MOSTLY   SORT OF   NOT AT ALL

1.

2.

3.

4.

5.

If I'm busy with good deeds,
the waiting will go quickly.
Here are some things I'm going to do
to make the time fly:

_____
_____
_____
_____
_____
_____
_____

When I think about Isaiah 40:30–31
and flying on the wings of eagles, I feel

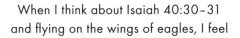

_____
_____
_____
_____
_____

The Most Exhausting Time of the Year

I think it probably goes without saying that *rest* is not a word most people use to describe Christmastime. It's almost laughable to think that rest would define the holiday season. When I think of the holidays, I think of hours of online shopping for the perfect Christmas gifts, scrambling to decorate my house, enjoying Christmas movies (both old and new), attending parties with friends and loved ones, late nights socializing or wrapping gifts, and a general feeling of excitement with a side of exhaustion. There's a madness that makes the season thrilling at times, but the crash on the other side is unavoidable.

As the years have gone by, my Christmas seasons have evolved. We no longer have tiny feet scampering down the hallway at 5:30 on Christmas morning, excited voices begging us to climb out of bed and check under the tree for gifts. I've learned in recent years to build in some weeks without work to enjoy being with friends and family without the pressure of filming schedules and work engagements. But somehow, the season still remains full and demanding. And I find myself exhausted.

Our society often measures our "success" during the holiday season by our accomplishments. How big was your party? How many presents did you creatively curate and wrap immaculately? Did you capture each moment in photos, caption them with something clever, and share them with all your followers? We are constantly drawn into the craziness and busyness of Christmastime.

I'm sure even reading that last paragraph set off a million reminders in your head of things you need to get to! But I hope a tiny voice inside your head is alerting you to the sadness around this type of insanity and pressure. Remind yourself today of Jesus' tender words in Matthew 11:28: "Come to me, all who labor and are heavy laden, and I will give you rest" (ESV). Read those words again and take a big, deep breath after reading them. Rest! Rest! Rest! That often-unattainable word promised to us by a Savior who sees us in the midst of our madness.

I wonder if part of Jesus coming to earth as a baby was to model that beautiful dependence on rest. Have you ever met a newborn who doesn't like to sleep? Jesus came to earth as a baby—the reason we celebrate Christmas—and guess what He probably did in the first hour of His life? He rested! He didn't show up as an energetic teenager, ready to take on the world or as a workaholic twenty-five-year-old. He showed up humbly, in need of care and rest as a newborn baby.

Unfortunately for most of us, three naps a day just aren't possible. We have our own people who depend on us. Maybe you have your own babies (big and small), a spouse, an aging parent, a boss, or employees who rely on you. We all have responsibilities and obligations that call our names in the middle of a busy season of life. But—don't miss this *but*—we also serve a God who offers us rest in the middle of a month that often takes all we have.

Think about the weeks ahead. About the parties to attend, the outfits to buy, the gifts to wrap, the treats to bake, the sleeplessness to overcome. Now take a big breath and remind yourself that the God you serve offers you rest. He calls you to "come to" Him and rest. To sit and do nothing. To take a nap. To read His Word. To stand in the shower for ten extra minutes. To go on a walk. To enjoy a cup of tea. To simply breathe in deeply and exhale. Make rest a part of your Christmas this year.

When the Stars of Morning Sang

by Anne P. L. Field

When the stars of morning sang
    Long ago,
Sweet the air with music rang
    Through the snow,
There beside the mother mild
    Slept the blessed Christmas child—
Slumber holy, undefiled—
    Here below.

When the wise men traveled far
    Through the night,
Following the guiding star
    Pure and bright,
Lo! it stood above the place
    Sanctified by Heaven's grace,
And upon the Christ Child's face
    Shed its light.

When the world lay hushed and still
    Christmas morn,
Suddenly were skies a'thrill—
    Christ is born!
Angel voices, high and clear,
    Chanted tidings of good cheer,
See, the Infant King is here,
    Christ is born!

Today is a rest day!

Nothing to fill in; nothing to think through or shade in. I want you to set a timer for fifteen minutes. Before you start, set your phone aside, grab your cozy drink of choice, and sit somewhere that will bring you calm. Just sit with Jesus for the next fifteen minutes and enjoy a time of peace and quiet. If it helps to focus you, read through some of the verses listed on these pages about Jesus bringing rest.

Come to me, all who labor and are heavy laden, and I will give you rest.

MATTHEW 11:28 (ESV)

Truly my soul finds rest in God; my salvation comes from Him.

PSALM 62:1 (NIV)

I will both lie down and sleep in peace, for you alone, LORD, make me live in safety.

PSALM 4:8 (CSB)

Whoever dwells
in the shelter
of the Most High
will rest in the shadow
of the Almighty.
I will say of the LORD,
"He is my refuge
and my fortress,
my God,
in whom I trust."

PSALM 91:1-2 (NIV)

Silent night! Holy night!
All is calm, all is bright
Round yon Virgin Mother and Child!
Holy infant, so tender and mild,
Sleep in heavenly peace!
Sleep in heavenly peace!
Silent night! Holy night!
Son of God, love's pure light
Radiant beams from Thy holy face,
With the dawn of redeeming grace,
Jesus, Lord at Thy birth!
Jesus, Lord at Thy birth!

—FROM "SILENT NIGHT" BY JOSEPH MOHR
(ENGLISH LYRICS BY JOHN FREEMAN YOUNG)

Never Alone

Have you ever found yourself at a party, surrounded by people but still feeling so alone? Have you ever gotten lost in a spiral of social media stalking, feeling like you are the only person who doesn't have a bustling social life? Loneliness is such a difficult feeling to navigate, especially during a holiday like Christmas. At Christmas it feels good to buy gifts for other people, invite friends over to celebrate, or attend church services with friends or family. We are wired for connectedness, and often the holidays can magnify something we deeply long for like relationships with others.

Even though you might be feeling alone, you are not alone! So many people experience loneliness even when they are surrounded by people. Maybe you are feeling misunderstood, desperate for someone to validate what you're going through. Perhaps you're feeling unseen and underappreciated after making the thousandth dinner for your family without so much as a "thanks, Mom." Or maybe you are truly physically alone this Christmas, longing for a hug from your mom or a coffee date with your best friend. Whatever your circumstances might be, I can promise you that you are not alone.

In Matthew 28:19, Jesus gives His disciples a great mission: "Go therefore and make disciples of all the nations" (NKJV). Can you imagine the weight of that calling? If I put myself in their shoes, I am completely and totally overwhelmed by the thought of being tasked with sharing the good news of Jesus with the whole world! But, of course, Jesus recognizes this incredible weight and reminds His disciples, "I am with you always, *even* to the end of the age" (MATTHEW 28:20 NKJV, EMPHASIS ADDED). He knows that the weight and burden of their task is only made lighter by His presence.

I wonder what burdens we carry that leave us feeling alone and overwhelmed. Sometimes grief pushes us to that point. Maybe you've gone through a terrible tragedy that you feel no one else can understand. If that's you, Jesus is with you always. Or maybe your thought life feels too vulnerable to share with another soul. If that's you, your shame is not too much because Jesus is with you always. Maybe you feel unwanted this Christmas, cast aside, or discarded. Dear friend, if that's you, Jesus is with you always.

This Christmas I urge you to look around and see that Jesus has not left you. Look for ways that He meets you, provides for you, sees you, and stays with you. Feel the deep reassurance that no matter the weight of your loneliness, you are truly not alone. Take this knowledge and let it spur you on to bring togetherness instead of isolation. Look for the woman on the street who could use a friend. Keep your eyes open for a friend who might be feeling similarly alone. Invite her in, share your home with her, create space for togetherness.

Believing the lie that we are alone can only keep us from following Jesus' call on our lives. Do you think that you cannot possibly find hope or community in the midst of your loneliness? Trust me here—that is just not true. Jesus offers you companionship in Him and access to a community of believers that will remind you that you truly belong. Look around for ways that you see Jesus in your own life and let it fuel you to be the hands and feet of Jesus in other people's lives. And remember, Jesus is with you *always*.

The Little Match Girl

by Hans Christian Andersen

(TRANSLATED AND ADAPTED)

It was very, very cold; it snowed and it grew dark; it was the last evening of the year, New Year's Eve. A poor little girl, with bare head and bare feet, was walking through the streets. In an old apron the little girl carried a number of matches, and a bundle of them in her hand. No one had bought anything from her all day; no one had given her a copper.

Her small hands were quite numb with the cold. Ah! A little match might do her good if she only dared draw one from the bundle and strike it against the wall and warm her fingers at it. She drew one out. *R-r-atch!* How it spluttered and burned! It was a warm, bright flame, like a little candle, when she held her hands over it. It really seemed to the little girl as if she sat before a great polished stove. The fire burned so nicely; it warmed her so well. The little girl was just putting out her feet to warm these, too, when out went the flame; the stove was gone. She sat with only the end of the burned match in her hand.

She struck another; it burned; it gave a light; and where it shone on the wall, the wall became thin like a veil, and she could see through it into the room where a table stood, spread with a white cloth, and with china on it;

and the roast goose smoked gloriously, stuffed with apples and dried plums. The goose hopped down from the dish and waddled along the floor, with a knife and fork in its breast; straight to the little girl he came. Then the match went out, and only the thick, damp, cold wall was before her.

She lighted another. Then she was sitting under a beautiful Christmas tree; it was greater and finer than the one she had seen through the glass door at the rich merchant's. Thousands of candles burned upon the green branches, and colored pictures like those in the shop windows looked down upon them. The little girl stretched forth both hands toward them; then the match went out. The Christmas lights went higher and higher. She saw that now they were stars in the sky; one of them fell and made a long line of fire.

"Now someone is dying," said the little girl, for her old grandmother, the only person who had been good to her, but who was now dead, had said, "When a star falls a soul mounts up to God."

She rubbed another match against the wall; it became bright again, and in the light there stood the old grandmother clear and shining, mild and lovely.

"Grandmother!" cried the child. "Oh, take me with you! I know you will go when the match is burned out. You will go away like the warm stove, the nice roast goose, and the great glorious Christmas tree!"

And she hastily rubbed the whole bundle of matches, for she wished to hold her grandmother fast. And the matches burned with such a glow that it became brighter than in the middle of the day. Grandmother had never been so large or so beautiful. She took the little girl up in her arms, and both flew in the light and the joy so high, so high! And up there was no cold, nor hunger, nor care—they were with God.

The New Year's sun rose upon the little body that sat there with the matches, of which one bundle was burned. She wanted to warm herself, the people said. No one knew what fine things she had seen and in what glory she had gone in with her grandmother to the New Year's Day.

Spend time in prayer using this guide.

Lord, only You know me fully.
There are moments I feel like I have no one with me.
I feel lonely when

_____

_____

_____

_____

_____

_____

_____

I know I'm not alone in my loneliness though.
There are others around me who are experiencing this as well.
I see loneliness when

_____

_____

_____

_____

_____

_____

_____

You tell me that You are always with me,
but sometimes I forget.
Please help me know that I am not alone because

_____

_____

_____

_____

_____

_____

_____

_____

_____

I want to be a part of creating spaces
where people feel known.
Give me the confidence to help create community by

_____

_____

_____

_____

_____

_____

_____

_____

_____

_____

Ultimately, let me feel Your presence and Your love.
Remind me that You are

_____

_____

_____

_____

_____

_____

_____

_____

_____

Away in a manger, no crib for a bed,
The little Lord Jesus laid down His sweet head.
The stars in the bright sky looked down where He lay—
The little Lord Jesus asleep on the hay.
The cattle are lowing, the baby awakes,
But little Lord Jesus, no crying He makes.
I love Thee, Lord Jesus! Look down from the sky,
And stay by my cradle till morning is nigh.

—FROM "CRADLE HYMN"
BY MARTIN LUTHER

Peace on Earth

One of my favorite names for Jesus is the Prince of Peace. Isaiah calls Jesus this when prophesying about the King who would one day come to earth. It seems that since the beginning of time, peace has eluded us. We seem to always be getting in our own way—saying or doing things that create conflict, putting ourselves above others, or sacrificing our love for others for our love for ourselves.

Peace is a quality that reflects the heart of God. In Galatians we read that one of the fruits of the Spirit is peace. Becoming more like God means you will have more peace. During the Christmas season, we sing carols and read Scriptures that remind us of this important word: "Peace on earth and mercy mild, God and sinners reconciled" (from "Hark the Herald Angels Sing") and "on earth peace, good will toward men" (LUKE 2:14 KJV). Peace is a crucial part of our faith as we grow and develop and reflect our Savior.

But how do we cultivate peace this Christmas season? In a world where peace often feels far away, how do we bring peace to our communities and our own hearts? Peace has been described as a feeling of completeness and harmony despite our circumstances. And don't we often find ourselves in circumstances that leave us feeling at odds or incomplete? This is such a normal part of our experience as people, so the elusive feeling of peace can often feel far off.

But be encouraged this Christmas season. Peace is available to you.

Leaning into the truths about who God says He is—unchanging, never-ending, always faithful, always true—can bring a deep sense of confidence in a world that is ever-changing. Paul writes in his letter to the Philippians that in moments of uncertainty, fear, or trial you can "present your requests to God. And the *peace* of God, which transcends all understanding, will guard your hearts and minds in Christ Jesus" (PHILIPPIANS 4:6-7 NIV, EMPHASIS ADDED).

I love that Paul acknowledges that God's peace transcends understanding. It doesn't make sense to us because it is unnatural. It's not normal to feel a confidence in God's goodness despite our lives feeling out of control and tumultuous. Having a calm spirit in the midst of a world that is ever changing and full of contentious opinions and conversations is something that we can only access through the peace of our heavenly Father.

Living a life of peace is not only beneficial because it puts us at ease, but Jesus also tells us that blessing accompanies making peace. In His Sermon on the Mount He says, "Blessed are the peacemakers, for they will be called children of God" (MATTHEW 5:9 NIV).

Do you see yourself as a child of God? As a bearer of peace? How can you develop this attitude this Christmas season?

How can you bring peace around the family dinner table? How can you emit peace to those who are suffering this Christmas? What peace can you cultivate for those who see things differently than you? What hardship might you encounter this Christmas season that can only be weathered through the peace of God?

I encourage you, sister, no matter what you encounter this holiday season, to present your requests to God! Spend time with Him, asking Him for supernatural peace to guard your heart and mind. Ask Him to not let fear, insecurity, anger, and grief overtake you. Ask Him to meet you in the middle of your circumstances with His overwhelming peace.

Little Christmas Carolers

by L. A. France

We are a band of carolers,
   We march through frost and snow,
But care not for the weather
   As on our way we go.

At every hall or cottage
   That stands upon our way,
We stop to give the people
   Best wishes for the day.

We pray a merry Christmas,
   Made bright by Christmas cheer,
With peace, and hope, and gladness
   And all they may hold dear.

And for all those that happen
   To pass us on our way
We have a smile, and wish them
   A merry Christmas Day.

Most of us will admit that this season of *giving* can also be a season of *asking*. Thankfully, the Bible encourages us to ask God in prayer for things we need—whether spiritual, physical, or emotional needs. Sometimes what we really need—especially during stressful times—is peace. Philippians 4:6–7 says, "Do not be anxious about anything, but in every situation, by prayer and petition, with thanksgiving, present your requests to God. And the peace of God, which transcends all understanding, will guard your hearts and your minds in Christ Jesus" (NIV). Think through these different categories and how you might need the peace of God in your life. Then take time to pray, and present your requests to God.

Family

FINISH EACH PRAYER ABOUT YOUR FAMILY

God, I worry about my family because _____

_____

I'm thankful to You for _____

_____

Fill my heart with peace during this Christmas season, and help me and my family _____

_____

Thank You for guarding my heart and my mind. Help me to feel Your presence when I _____

_____

_____

Work

FINISH EACH PRAYER
ABOUT YOUR WORK

God, I worry about my work because _____

_____

I'm thankful to You for _____

_____

Fill my heart with peace during this Christmas season, and help me and my coworkers _____

_____

_____

Thank You for guarding my heart and my mind. Help me to feel Your presence when I

_____

_____

Friends

God, I worry about my friends because _____

_____

I'm thankful to You for _____

_____

Fill my heart with peace during this Christmas season, and help me and my friends to _____

_____

Thank You for guarding my heart and my mind. Help me to feel Your presence when I _____

_____

In the world

God, I worry about the world because _____

_____

I'm thankful to You for _____

_____

Fill my heart with peace during this Christmas season, and help me to _____

_____

Thank You for guarding my heart and my mind. Help me to feel Your presence when I _____

_____

For myself

FINISH EACH PRAYER ABOUT YOURSELF

God, I worry about my life because _____
_____
_____

I'm thankful to You for _____

_____
_____

Fill my heart with peace during this Christmas season, and help me to _____
_____
_____

Thank You for guarding my heart and my mind. Help me to feel Your presence when I _____
_____
_____

Beauty from Ashes

Since I can remember, I've felt insecure about my voice. Seems silly, right? People would comment that it was high-pitched, squeaky, even annoying. And in my profession, that's not really feedback anyone wants to hear! I would try to talk in a lower register and constantly feel self-conscious and embarrassed about how I sounded. In the last couple of years, though, I started reading Scripture out loud on my social media accounts, and something amazing happened. Sweet viewers started messaging me saying, "I could listen to you all day long." These messages brought me to tears—and not because of the praise but because of the incredible ability Jesus has to redeem the parts of life that bring us the most shame.

We all carry insecurities with us. Some of us might be insecure about what we look like; we worry that our curly locks appear less professional than the long, straight-hair look, or maybe we're troubled by the smile lines that have recently appeared on our face. For some, it might be our careers or financial status that cause us to cringe. For some, struggles with addiction might bring up feelings of shame. We so often hear what we *should* be like. We receive messages on social media or even within our own communities that try to tell us what makes us valuable. This lens will ultimately leave us feeling discontent and never-enough. We will be pulled into the cycle of constantly striving for bigger and better.

Paul writes this encouragement to the Romans: "We know that in all things God works for the good of those who love Him, who have been called according to His purpose" (ROMANS 8:28 NIV). If you love God, be encouraged! God is working in all things for your good. He does not work for your embarrassment or your ruin—God works for your good! He is a God who works within our limitations, our struggles, our failures and brings about good. He is not bound by our willingness and surrender; God does not bring about redemption because of anything we facilitate. Our insecurities and shortcomings cannot stop God from bringing about good.

Think about what you work hard to hide or change in your own life. Can you imagine if that part of your life that you despise became an instrument of bringing about glory to your heavenly Father? If that area that you try to run from actually helped others run to the arms of God? This is the power of a Savior who redeems.

Think today about what Christmas means. Christmas is the beginning of a story of redemption. It's the start of the life of the man who brought about ultimate redemption. When Jesus came to earth, He came in a humble, low position. Throughout His entire life, He put Himself in places where He was subject to mockery, humiliation, and shame. But these areas that Jesus stepped into, He always worked for good. How can you take a step toward a new life that is geared toward redemption? What area of your life can you invite Jesus into? What do you want to ask Him to transform? How can you open your eyes to the redemptive work God is already doing in your life?

The verse in Romans reminds us that God works for our good *in all areas* of our lives. Not just some areas. Not the areas that we're ready to give up. Not just the areas that seem simple. God will work in all things! God is not done with you. He has plans for good and for beauty. He is a God of transformation and redemption. Today, surrender those areas and ask to be part of the process of redeeming brokenness!

How the Fir Tree Became the Christmas Tree

by Aunt Hede

This is the story of how the fir tree became the Christmas tree.

At the time when the Christ Child was born, all the people, the animals, and the trees and plants were very happy. The Child was born to bring peace and happiness to the whole world. People came daily to see the little One, and they always brought gifts with them.

There were three trees standing near the crypt, and they wished that they, too, might give presents to the Christ Child.

The Palm said, "I will choose my most beautiful leaf and place it as a fan over the Child."

"And I," said the Olive, "will sprinkle sweet-smelling oil upon His head."

"What can I give to the Child?" asked the Fir, who stood near.

"You?" cried the others. "You have nothing to offer Him. Your needles would prick Him, and your tears are sticky."

So, the poor little Fir tree was very unhappy, and it said, "Yes, you are right. I have nothing to offer the Christ Child."

Now, quite near the trees stood the Christmas Angel, who had heard all that the trees had said. The Angel was sorry for the Fir tree who was so lowly and without envy of the other trees. So, when it was dark and the stars came out, he begged a few of the little stars to come down and rest upon the branches of the Fir tree. They did as the Christmas Angel asked, and the Fir tree shone suddenly with a beautiful light.

And at that very moment, the Christ Child opened His eyes—for He had been asleep—and as the lovely light fell upon Him, He smiled.

Every year people keep the dear Christmas Child's birthday by giving gifts to each other. And every year, in remembrance of His first birthday, the Christmas Angel places in every house a fir tree. Covered with starry candles, it shines for the children as the stars shone for the Christ Child. The Fir tree was rewarded for its meekness, for to no other tree is it given to shine upon so many happy faces.

Take some time to think through how God made you and how you could use your gifts and unique qualities for the kingdom of God.

Words that describe me

- ☐ Creative
- ☐ Intellectual
- ☐ Serious
- ☐ Excitable
- ☐ Introverted
- ☐ Extraverted

- ☐ Kind
- ☐ Lighthearted
- ☐ Hardworking
- ☐ Wise
- ☐ Other:_____
- ☐ Other:_____

How I love to spend my free time

- ☐ Reading
- ☐ Watching TV
- ☐ Cooking
- ☐ Exercising
- ☐ Talking with friends

- ☐ Decorating my home
- ☐ Writing letters
- ☐ Other:_____
- ☐ Other:_____
- ☐ Other:_____

What makes me feel loved

- ☐ Kind words
- ☐ Hugs
- ☐ When someone folds my laundry
- ☐ Coffee dates
- ☐ A thoughtful gift
- ☐ When someone listens to me
- ☐ Other:_____
- ☐ Other:_____

Ways I think God made me to help build His kingdom

- ☐ Teaching others about God
- ☐ Hosting people in my home
- ☐ Caring for children
- ☐ Leading a Bible study
- ☐ Serving in my church
- ☐ Praying for others
- ☐ Other:_____
- ☐ Other:_____
- ☐ Other:_____

Where I enjoy talking to God

- [ ] In nature
- [ ] By my fireplace
- [ ] At church
- [ ] On a walk
- [ ] Cozy in my bed
- [ ] Other:_____
- [ ] Other:_____
- [ ] Other:_____

What motivates me

- [ ] Someone encouraging me
- [ ] Taking a risk
- [ ] External incentives
- [ ] Someone pushing me
- [ ] Other:_____
- [ ] Other:_____

People who love me well

- [ ] _____
- [ ] _____
- [ ] _____
- [ ] _____
- [ ] _____
- [ ] _____
- [ ] _____
- [ ] _____
- [ ] _____
- [ ] _____

Our God, heaven cannot hold Him
Nor earth sustain;
Heaven and earth shall flee away
When He comes to reign.
In the bleak midwinter
A stable-place sufficed
The Lord God Almighty—
Jesus Christ. . . .
What can I give Him,
Poor as I am?
If I were a shepherd
I would bring a lamb,
If I were a Wise Man,
I would do my part,
—Yet what I can I give Him,
Give my heart.

—FROM "IN THE BLEAK MIDWINTER"
BY CHRISTINA G. ROSSETTI

Wonder and Amazement

Imagine the look on a child's face on Christmas morning. The glee, the bliss, the crazed, twinkly eyes and audible screams! There is something sacred about the wonderment children feel when they encounter that majestic tree on Christmas morning. They stare in amazement at the incredible gifts and wonder where all the presents came from! I wish I could capture all they feel in that moment and bottle it up. I would let it out in little bursts throughout my year, fueling me and propelling me forward with the joy and excitement that only children can harness.

As we grow up, we start to lose that childlike wonder and awe. As kids, beauty so easily moved us: the sight of a colorful flower, a tiny caterpillar, a full moon, Mom all dressed up for a date with Daddy. Each of these simple sights brought joy and amazement. It brought us back to a God who loves to create beautiful things!

We have an opportunity to experience the joy of creation if we open our eyes to observe all the beauty around us. Psalm 19:1 tells us that "the heavens proclaim the glory of God. The skies display His craftsmanship" (NLT). Creation points us to the incredible creativity of God.

Wonder has another side, though, that we can't miss! Wonder instructs us not only to marvel at and revel in but also to question, to be curious and hungry to know and experience the world. One Christmas song gives us words for this sort of thinking: "I wonder as I wander out under the sky."* The author of this song poses one of the most important questions surrounding the Christmas story: "I wonder . . . how Jesus the Savior did come for to die . . .?"*

I love this question because it gets at the heart of the word *wonder*. The wondering and the questioning are done with a heart of amazement and curiosity instead of doubt. It leads us to marvel at God's incredible mercy and goodness to us. I've often asked my kids, "How can I love you so much?" I sit amazed at the depth of love I have for my three beautiful kids. Wondering is cultivating a spirit of gratitude and proclaiming the blessings that God gives us.

What do you have to marvel at this Christmas season? What blessings has God placed in your life that you might need to stop and consider? Are you experiencing a season of great joy or celebration in your life? Tell someone! Thank God for this season. Perhaps the blessings are less obvious this year. Maybe you need to open up that bottle of childlike wonder and stop to consider a beautiful snow-covered tree outside your window. Maybe looking over letters or Christmas cards from past years will inspire a feeling of thankfulness for all the people who love and care for you. Maybe a quiet evening around the fireplace reading a good book is what your soul needs to cultivate this sort of wonder.

Stop to enjoy the wonder that is infused into Christmas. Remind yourself that wonderment at Christmastime doesn't have to hinge on material things. Look around you and wonder at the physical body God gave you to enjoy life with. Thank Him for the roof over your head, an invigorating sip of coffee, the Christmas ornament that reminds you of your mom. Wonder is available all around you—open your eyes and soak it in!

---

*   "I Wonder as I Wander" by John Jacob Niles (1933).

Little Piccola

by Celia Thaxter

In the sunny land of France there lived many years ago a sweet little maid named Piccola.

Her father had died when she was a baby, and her mother was very poor and had to work hard all day in the fields for a few sous.

Little Piccola had no dolls or toys, and she was often hungry and cold, but she was never sad nor lonely.

So what if there were no children for her to play with! So what if she did not have fine clothes and beautiful toys! In summer there were always the birds in the forest and the flowers in the fields and meadows—the birds sang so sweetly, and the flowers were so bright and pretty!

In the winter when the ground was covered with snow, Piccola helped her mother and knit long stockings of blue wool. The snowbirds had to be fed with crumbs, if she could find any, and then there was Christmas Day.

But one year her mother was ill and could not earn any money. Piccola worked hard all day long and sold the stockings that she knit, even when her own little bare feet were blue with the cold.

As Christmas Day drew near, she said to her mother, "I wonder what the good Saint Nicholas will bring me this year. I cannot hang my stocking in the fireplace, but I shall put my wooden shoe on the hearth for him. He will not forget me, I am sure."

"Do not think of it this year, my dear child," replied her mother. "We must be glad if we have bread enough to eat."

But Piccola could not believe that the good saint would forget her. On Christmas Eve she put her little wooden patten on the hearth before the fire and went to sleep to dream of Saint Nicholas.

As the poor mother looked at the little shoe, she thought how unhappy her dear child would be to find it empty in the morning and wished that she had something, even if it were only a tiny cake, for a Christmas gift. There was nothing in the house but a few sous, and these must be saved to buy bread.

When the morning dawned, Piccola awoke and ran to her shoe.

Saint Nicholas had come in the night. He had not forgotten the little child who had thought of him with such faith. See what he had brought her. It lay in the wooden patten, looking up at her with its two bright eyes and chirping contentedly as she stroked its soft feathers. A little swallow, cold and hungry, had flown into the chimney and down to the room; it had crept into the shoe for warmth.

Piccola danced for joy and clasped the shivering swallow to her breast.

She ran to her mother's bedside. "Look, look!" she cried. "A Christmas gift, a gift from the good Saint Nicholas!" And she danced again in her little bare feet.

Then she fed and warmed the bird, and cared for it tenderly all winter long, teaching it to take crumbs from her hand and her lips and to sit on her shoulder while she was working.

In the spring she opened the window for it to fly away, but it lived in the woods nearby all summer, and it came often in the early morning to sing its sweetest songs at her door.

When and where do you feel the wonderment of God?
Fill in the chart below.

WHEN I FEEL WONDERMENT	WHERE I FEEL WONDERMENT

What gets in the way of you experiencing the awe and wonder of the Christmas season? *(Check all that apply.)*

☐ Financial pressure

☐ Family issues

☐ Busyness of the season

☐ Missing how things used to be

☐ Loss of a loved one

What are some other things that are getting in the way of you delighting in the season this Christmas?

_____

_____

_____

_____

Where are you going to seek awe and wonderment this holiday season?

SHADE IN THE ICONS

Nature

Family

Fireplace

Decorating

Bible

Christmas Card

Where else can you seek awe and wonderment?
Draw those places here.

How can I make time to marvel in the week ahead? *Fill out the graph below and add in a few hours this week to sit in the awe and amazement of Jesus' birth.*

EXAMPLE

EXAMPLE

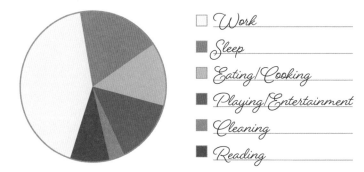

☐ *Work* _____

■ *Sleep* _____

■ *Eating/Cooking* _____

■ *Playing/Entertainment*

■ *Cleaning* _____

■ *Reading* _____

YOUR TURN   KEY

☐ _____

☐ _____

☐ _____

☐ _____

☐ _____

☐ _____

☐ _____

There's a song in the air!
There's a star in the sky!
There's a mother's deep prayer
And a baby's low cry!
And the star rains its fire while the Beautiful sing,
For the manger of Bethlehem cradles a king.
There's a tumult of joy
O'er the wonderful birth,
For the virgin's sweet boy
Is the Lord of the earth.
Ay! the star rains its fire and the Beautiful sing,
For the manger of Bethlehem cradles a king.

—FROM "THERE'S A SONG IN THE AIR"
BY JOSIAH GILBERT HOLLAND

Hall of Heroes

My family and I enjoy watching a good Christmas movie. It adds to the Christmas magic, gets us in the mood to celebrate, and always is full of sweet nostalgia. We all have our favorite Christmas movie heroes. Maybe you're drawn toward sweet Cindy Lou Who, whose tenderness helped grow the Grinch's heart two sizes! Maybe you relate more to George Bailey—a bit lost and aimless, disappointed by your circumstances, but ready to find a new outlook on life. Perhaps Buddy the Elf's joy-filled existence speaks to you and encourages you to enjoy everything from a cup of coffee to a plate full of spaghetti and syrup. We all have our favorite Christmas heroes and heroines; each one stands out for different reasons, but each brings us joy at Christmastime.

Finding people who inspire us to live better lives can be a really helpful tool in spurring on our spiritual growth. The more you study Scripture, the more and more you find people throughout history who not only lived good lives but lived Spirit-filled lives. People who changed the course of human history because of their obedience and willingness to trust God with difficult circumstances. One chapter of the Bible that really focuses on the heroes of faith is Hebrews 11. This chapter is often referred to as the "Hall of Faith" because the author of Hebrews outlines the incredible faith of many people throughout the Bible all in one chapter.

Many of these people came from ordinary circumstances and struggled in one form or another. The quality, though, that binds each of these incredible people together is faith. Over and over again, the author of Hebrews emphasizes that it was *by faith* that these heroes lived and acted.

I urge you to imagine what your life would look like if you lived *by faith*. What, *by faith*, might God use you to accomplish? What plan could you participate in? What legacy could you leave? What person could you impact?

Faith can be a difficult word to navigate. The first verse of Hebrews 11 tells us that "faith is confidence in what we hope for and assurance about what we do not see" (NIV). Faith is based on not seeing but having confidence in a hope, not a current reality.

All throughout Scripture, we see these heroes taking risks because they believed the promises of God. These ordinary people were used in extraordinary ways because they set aside their own comfort and reputation and said *yes* to the call of God in their lives.

This Christmas, you are capable of saying that same *yes*. What, by faith, could you step into for the sake of furthering your Maker's kingdom? Look beyond our beloved Christmas movie heroes, and pursue a life of meaning and impact that is rooted in God's character and goodness. The author of Hebrews tells readers at the end of the chapter that all the heroes of faith "were approved through their faith" (HEBREWS 11:39 CSB).

This is such good news for us! We are a part of a family and a lineage of heroic, faith-filled believers who acted obediently in faith and set an example for us so that we can grow in obedience and faith. We now have the chance to act in that same faith to impact the faith of generations to come. What, by faith, will you do today to be a hero of faith to those around you?

The Three Purses

by *William S. Walsh* (ADAPTED)

When Saint Nicholas was Bishop of Myra, there were among his people three beautiful maidens, daughters of a nobleman. Their father was so poor that he could not afford to give them dowries, and as in that land no maid might marry without a dowry, so these three maidens could not wed the youths who loved them.

At last the father became so very poor that he no longer had money with which to buy food or clothes for his daughters, and he was overcome by shame and sorrow. As for the daughters, they wept continually, for they were both cold and hungry.

One day Saint Nicholas heard of the sad state of this noble family. So at night, when the maidens were asleep and the father was watching, sorrowful and lonely, the good saint took a handful of gold and, tying it in a purse, set off for the nobleman's house. Creeping to the open window, he threw the purse into the chamber so that it fell on the bed of the sleeping maidens.

The father picked up the purse, and when he opened it and saw the gold, he rejoiced greatly and awakened his daughters. He gave most of the gold to his eldest child for a dowry, and thus she was enabled to wed the young man she loved.

A few days later Saint Nicholas filled another purse with gold and, as before, went by night to the nobleman's house and tossed the purse through the open window. Thus, the second daughter was enabled to marry the young man she loved.

Now, the nobleman felt very grateful to the unknown one who threw purses of gold into his room, and he longed to know who his benefactor was and to thank him. So the next night he watched beneath the open window. And when all was dark, lo! good Saint Nicholas came for the third time, carrying a silken purse filled with gold, and as he was about to throw it on the youngest maiden's bed, the nobleman caught him by his robe, crying, "Oh, good Saint Nicholas! Why do you hide yourself thus?"

And he kissed the saint's hands and feet, but Saint Nicholas, overcome with confusion at having his good deed discovered, begged the nobleman to tell no man what had happened.

Thus, the nobleman's third daughter was enabled to marry the young man she loved, and she and her father and her two sisters lived happily for the remainder of their lives.

Read Hebrews 11 (NIV)

Now faith is confidence in what we hope for and assurance about what we do not see. This is what the ancients were commended for. By faith we understand that the universe was formed at God's command, so that what is seen was not made out of what was visible. By faith Abel brought God a better offering than Cain did. By faith he was commended as righteous, when God spoke well of his offerings. And by faith Abel still speaks, even though he is dead. By faith Enoch was taken from this life, so that he did not experience death: "He could not be found, because God had taken him away." For before he was taken, he was commended as one who pleased God. And without faith it is impossible to please God, because anyone who comes to Him must believe that He exists and that He rewards those who earnestly seek Him.

By faith Noah, when warned about things not yet seen, in holy fear built an ark to save his family. By his faith he condemned the world and became heir of the righteousness that is in keeping with faith.

By faith Abraham, when called to go to a place he would later receive as his inheritance, obeyed and went, even though he did not know where he was going. By faith he made his home in the promised land like a stranger in a foreign country; he lived in tents, as did Isaac and Jacob, who were heirs with him of the same promise. For he was looking forward to the city with foundations, whose architect and builder is God. And by faith even Sarah, who was past childbearing age, was enabled to bear children because she considered him faithful who had made the promise. And so from this one man, and he as good as dead, came descendants as numerous as the stars in the sky and as countless as the sand on the seashore.

All these people were still living by faith when they died. They did not receive the things promised; they only saw them and welcomed them from a distance, admitting that they were foreigners and strangers on earth. People who say such things show that they are looking for a country of their own. If they had been thinking of the country they had left, they would have had opportunity to return. Instead, they were longing for a better country—a heavenly one. Therefore God is not ashamed to be called their God, for He has prepared a city for them.

By faith Abraham, when God tested him, offered Isaac as a sacrifice. He who had embraced the promises was about to sacrifice his one and only son, even though God had said to him, "It is through Isaac that your offspring will be reckoned." Abraham reasoned that God could even raise the dead, and so in a manner of speaking he did receive Isaac back from death.

By faith Isaac blessed Jacob and Esau in regard to their future.

By faith Jacob, when he was dying, blessed each of Joseph's sons, and worshiped as he leaned on the top of his staff.

By faith Joseph, when his end was near, spoke about the exodus of the Israelites from Egypt and gave instructions concerning the burial of his bones.

By faith Moses' parents hid him for three months after he was born, because they saw he was no ordinary child, and they were not afraid of the king's edict.

By faith Moses, when he had grown up, refused to be known as the son of Pharaoh's daughter. He chose to be mistreated along with the people of God rather than to enjoy the fleeting pleasures of sin. He regarded disgrace for the sake of Christ as of greater value than the treasures of Egypt, because he was looking ahead to his reward. By faith he left Egypt, not fearing the king's anger; he persevered because he saw him who is invisible. By faith he kept the Passover and the application of blood, so that the destroyer of the firstborn would not touch the firstborn of Israel.

By faith the people passed through the Red Sea as on dry land; but when the Egyptians tried to do so, they were drowned.

By faith the walls of Jericho fell, after the army had marched around them for seven days.

By faith the prostitute Rahab, because she welcomed the spies, was not killed with those who were disobedient.

And what more shall I say? I do not have time to tell about Gideon, Barak, Samson and Jephthah, about David and Samuel and the prophets, who through faith conquered kingdoms, administered justice, and gained what was promised; who shut the mouths of lions, quenched the fury of the flames, and escaped the edge of the sword; whose weakness was turned to strength; and who became powerful in battle and routed foreign armies. Women received back their dead, raised to life again. There were others who were tortured, refusing to be released so that they might gain an even better resurrection. Some faced jeers and flogging, and even chains and imprisonment. They were put to death by stoning; they were sawed in two; they were killed by the sword. They went about in sheepskins and goatskins, destitute, persecuted and mistreated— the world was not worthy of them. They wandered in deserts and mountains, living in caves and in holes in the ground.

These were all commended for their faith, yet none of them received what had been promised, since God had planned something better for us so that only together with us would they be made perfect.

What did these heroes do to show their faith?

ABEL	
NOAH	
ABRAHAM	
SARAH	
MOSES	
THE ISRAELITES	
RAHAB	

Who are your heroes? What makes them heroes?

YOUR HEROES	REASONS THEY ARE HEROES

What could you do *by faith?*

_____

_____

_____

_____

_____

Who or what has God placed in front of you, and how might you need to respond to that person or circumstance *by faith?*

_____

_____

_____

_____

_____

Finding Joy in Hard Circumstances

It's easy to get swept up in the merriment of the season only to come face-to-face with the reality that life is hard. Sometimes it feels like the joy that comes with Christmas should be able to cover over the hardships and sufferings of our everyday life. In some ways, though, the holiday season often amplifies our pain. In the midst of opening gifts, we can't help but notice the spot on the couch that is now empty after a devastating loss this year. We feel the pressure of gift giving in the midst of unemployment. We scroll through posts of happy families and cry over the conflict that defines our own family gatherings.

Suffering is a reality of our life here on earth. Our bodies fail us, old habits ruin the hope of new traditions, and the reality of the world's brokenness robs us of pure joy on Christmas. But friends, this is not a reality God didn't anticipate. Nothing we do and nothing we feel surprises Him. I find comfort in that. I hope you do too.

In Matthew 1:23, the angel tells Joseph in a dream that Jesus would be called "Immanuel, which means 'God is with us'" (NLT). God promised us a Savior who would be *with* us. Who would not leave us alone. He would suffer with us, grieve with us, encounter pain with us. How sweet to have a heavenly Father who knows the importance of the word *with*.

As you anticipate your Christmas plans, don't believe the painful lie that you are alone in your suffering. No matter what grief you might carry with you this holiday season, know fully that you are not alone.

Think about what difficulties you might encounter this Christmas and carry those to Jesus. Are you dreading Christmas dinner, where controversial topics and strong opinions are sure to destroy a joy-filled meal? Are you in the middle of walking through grief—maybe the end of a dream or the loss of a loved one—and feel the deep ache of what could have been? Are you grieving tension in a friendship and wishing for the lighthearted conversation and jokes that you shared not so long ago? Are you feeling the weight of loneliness in a season filled with togetherness?

Sister, you are not alone.

You are not alone in your suffering, your anxiety, your anger, your loneliness, your grief. You were created by a heavenly Father who knows you inside and out. By a Father who cherishes you from head to toe. A Father who hurts with you. A Father who sent His own Son to be "God with you" this holiday season.

Joy in the Christmas season can be deceiving. It can leave us feeling like we should skip through each day with a smile on our face and a twinkle in our eye. But that is just simply not the reality of a broken world. We each come into the holiday season with our own unique brand of suffering. Maybe this Christmas your trials are small or maybe they seem insurmountable. Wherever you find yourself, know that the joy of life with Christ is a sweeter joy than you can find anywhere else.

This is a joy that allows for an imperfect life. For tear-filled conversations with friends, for lonely shopping outings, for frustrating dinners with friends and family members. The joy we find in Jesus is one that runs deeper than circumstances because it provides a deep and lasting satisfaction in the knowledge that we are fiercely loved, seen, cherished, understood, and saved by a good God, a God who is with us. A God who does not leave us alone. *Ever.*

The Elves and the Shoemaker

by *Horace E. Scudder* (ADAPTED)

There was once a shoemaker who worked very hard and was honest. Still, he could not earn enough to live on. At last, all he had in the world was gone except just enough leather to make one pair of shoes. He cut these out at night and meant to rise early the next morning to make them up.

His heart was light in spite of his troubles, for his conscience was clear. He went quietly to bed, left all his cares to God, and fell asleep. In the morning he said his prayers and sat down to work, when, to his great wonder, there stood the shoes, already made, upon the table.

The good man knew not what to say or think. He looked at the work. There was not one false stitch in the whole job. All was neat and true.

That day a customer came in, and the shoes pleased him so well that he paid a price higher than usual for them. The shoemaker took the money and bought leather to make two pairs more. He cut out the work in the evening and went to bed early. He wished to be up with the sun and get to work.

When he got up in the morning, the work again was done. Soon buyers came in who paid him well for his goods. So, he bought leather enough for four pairs more.

He cut out the work again overnight and found it finished in the morning as before. So it went on for some time. What he got ready at night was always done by daybreak, and the good man soon was well-to-do.

One evening, at Christmastime, he and his wife sat over the fire, chatting, and he said, "I should like to sit up and watch tonight, that we may see who it is that comes and does my work for me." So, they left the light burning and hid behind a curtain to watch.

At midnight, there came two little elves. They sat upon the shoemaker's bench, stitching and rapping and tapping at such a rate that the shoemaker was amazed; he could not take his eyes off them.

They worked till the shoes were finished. Then they ran away as quick as lightning.

The next day the wife said to the shoemaker, "These little elves have made us rich, and we ought to thank them and do them some good in return. I am vexed to see them run about as they do. They have nothing upon their backs to keep off the cold. I will make each of them a shirt, and a coat and waistcoat, and a pair of pantaloons. You make each of them a little pair of shoes."

The good shoemaker liked the thought very well. One evening he and his wife had the clothes ready and placed them on the table instead of the work they used to cut out. Then they hid behind the curtain to watch what the little elves would do.

At midnight the elves came in and were going to sit down at their work as usual. But when they saw the clothes lying there for them, they laughed and were in high glee. They dressed themselves in the twinkling of an eye, and danced and capered and sprang about till at last they danced out the door and over the green.

The shoemaker saw them no more, but everything went well with him as long as he lived.

One of the names that Jesus receives is Immanuel: God *with* us.
Think back on your own life and journey. Then, in the boxes,
write down times you knew God was with you.

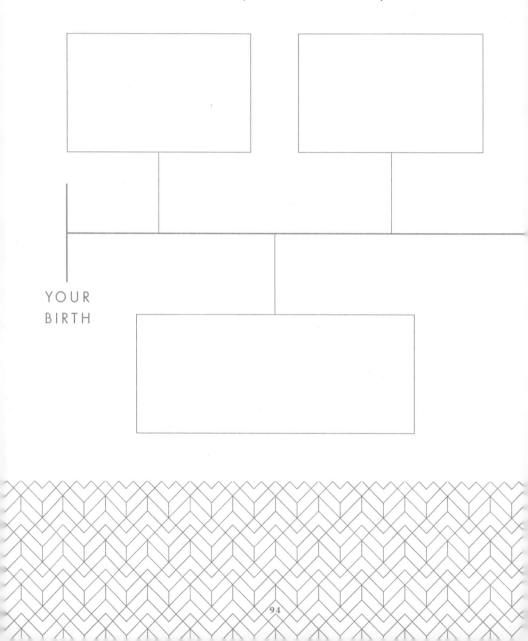

YOUR
BIRTH

Think about your life right now. How do you see God with you
in your current circumstances?

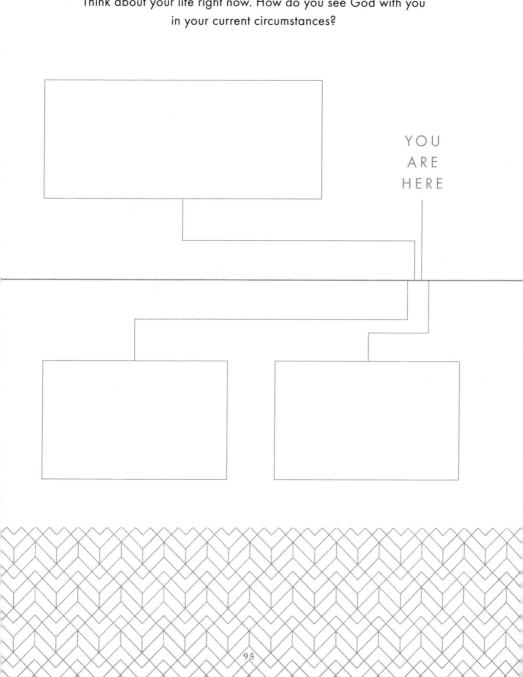

YOU
ARE
HERE

Imagine what's to come this Christmas or beyond.
Write a few prayers asking God to remind you that
He will be with you in what's to come.

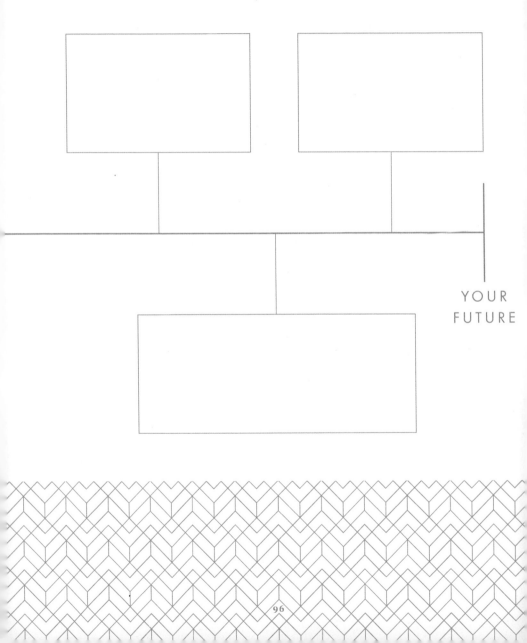

YOUR
FUTURE

Once in royal David's city
Stood a lowly cattle-shed
Where a mother laid her Baby,
In a manger for His bed.
Mary was that mother mild,
Jesus Christ her little Child.
He came down to earth from heaven,
Who is God and Lord of all,
And His shelter was a stable,
And His cradle was a stall.
With the poor, and mean, and lowly
Lived on earth our Savior holy.

—FROM "ONCE IN ROYAL DAVID'S CITY"
BY C. FRANCES ALEXANDER

Fear Not

Christmas doesn't typically feel like a time marked by fear. I mean, no one sits down to watch a feel-good Christmas movie expecting a horror film! Instead, we think of merriment, excitement, warmth, and joy surrounding the holidays. But the first Christmas was marked by a series of "Fear not" moments. The angel told Mary not to fear when she was pregnant. Joseph needed reminding to not be afraid to take Mary as his wife. The angel told the shepherds, "Do not be afraid." Fear is all throughout the story of Jesus' birth. It's okay to acknowledge this part of life even though the season of Christmas often feels like a time to avoid feelings of fear for the sake of merriment.

What I love about following God is that He never asks us to leave those things at the door. Instead, He sends reminders to His children to not be afraid. This Christmas, what makes your heart race? What makes your stomach turn over? What are you afraid of? Does the state of the world make you feel afraid? Does the safety or health of a loved one make you feel afraid? Are there threats to your career, your home, your mental health that make you feel afraid? I encourage you to cast these fears onto your heavenly Father.

God does not reply to these fears with "Fear not" because He doesn't care. He offers a "Fear not" because He has the confidence that life is more than just our earthly troubles. We are offered a life without fear because our life is no longer about the comforts and realities of this world alone. In Psalm

27:1, David wrote, "The LORD is my light and my salvation—whom shall I fear? The LORD is the stronghold of my life—of whom shall I be afraid?" (NIV).

The antidote to fear this Christmas is not to set it aside until the new year or to find a life that exists without things that make us afraid. Instead, the antidote to fear is the light offered by salvation. When things make me feel afraid, I remember my future—as well as my present—is secure in Jesus. I remember that I no longer have to carry my burdens alone. The light of Jesus' life casts out the darkness that so often closes in on us. Are you walking in the light? Do you feel the brightness and hope that a relationship with Jesus brings? Have you brought your fears into the light?

If you are afraid of failing, bring this into the light. If you are afraid of being honest about your own struggles, bring this into the light. If you are afraid of being accepted for your full self, bring this into the light. If you are afraid of being a disappointment, let the light of God's love for you wash over this fear. The love of God is available for all. His salvation is available to you because of what Jesus did on the cross, and this is the sort of love that casts out fear.

David asked, "Of whom shall I be afraid?" (PSALM 27:1 NIV). I ask you this same question today. There is no person, no circumstance, no outcome that will escape God. He is all-knowing and all-powerful. He loves deeply and compassionately. Bring your fears to God today and step into a life without fear because of the strength and peace we find in Him. Let the words that the angel spoke to Mary, Joseph, and the shepherds so long ago wash over you today: "Do not be afraid!"

A Christmas Fairy

by John Strange Winter

It was getting very near to Christmastime, and all the boys at Miss Ware's school were talking about going home for the holidays.

"I am going to stay here. I can't go home to India," answered Tom in a very forlorn voice.

"Poor fellow!" said Bertie Fellows. "If I couldn't go home for the holidays, especially at Christmas, I think I would just sit down and die."

"Oh no, you wouldn't," said Tom. "You would get ever so homesick, but you wouldn't die. You would just get through somehow and hope something would happen before next year, or that some kind fairy would—"

"There are no fairies nowadays," said Bertie. "See here, Tom, I'll write and ask my mother to invite you to go home with me for the holidays." In a few days' time a letter arrived from Bertie's mother. The boy opened it eagerly. It said:

My own dear Bertie:

I am very sorry to tell you that little Alice is ill with scarlet fever. And so you cannot come for your holidays. I would have been glad to have you bring your little friend with you if all had been well here.

—Your own mother

When Bertie received this letter, which ended all his Christmas hopes and joys, he hid his face upon his desk and sobbed aloud. The lonely boy from India, who sat next to him, tried to comfort his friend in every way he could think of. He patted his shoulder and whispered many kind words to him.

Miss Ware, smiling down on the two boys, said, "Poor Tom has been expecting to spend his holidays alone, and now he will have a friend with him. Try to look on the bright side, Bertie, and to remember how much worse it would have been if there had been no boy to stay with you."

The last day of the term came, and one by one, or two by two, the boys went away, until only Bertie and Tom were left in the great house. It had never seemed so large to either of them before. The evening passed, and the two boys went to bed. They told stories to each other for a long time before they could go to sleep. That night they dreamed of their homes and felt very lonely. Yet each tried to be brave, and so another day began.

This was the day before Christmas. Quite early in the morning came a great box from Bertie's mother. Then, just as dinner had come to an end, there was a peal of the bell, and a voice was heard asking for Tom Egerton. Tom sprang to his feet and flew to greet a tall, handsome lady, crying, "Aunt Laura! Aunt Laura!"

Laura explained that she and her husband had arrived in London only the day before. "I was so afraid, Tom," she said, "that we should not get here until Christmas Day was over and that you would be disappointed. So I would not let your mother write you that we were on our way home. You must get your things packed up at once and go back with me to London. Then uncle and I will give you a splendid time."

For a minute or two Tom's face shone with delight. Then he caught sight of Bertie and turned to his aunt. "Dear Aunt Laura," he said, "I am very sorry, but I can't leave Bertie here all alone. When I was going to be alone he wrote and asked his mother to let me go home with him. She could not have either of us because Bertie's sister has scarlet fever. He has to stay here, and he has never been away from home at Christmastime before, and I can't go away and leave him by himself, Aunt Laura."

For a minute Aunt Laura looked at the boy as if she could not believe him. Then she caught him in her arms and kissed him. "You dear little boy, you shall not leave him. You shall bring him along, and we shall all enjoy ourselves together. Bertie, my boy, you are not very old yet, but I am going to teach you a lesson as well as I can. It is that kindness is never wasted in this world."

And so Bertie and Tom found that there was such a thing as a fairy after all.

This Christmas, let joy overcome fear in your life. Sometimes the most helpful way to address fear is to first acknowledge the fear you've experienced in the past. Maybe you were afraid about something in the past—and then it turned out that there was nothing to be afraid of. Or maybe you received comfort and strength from God and were able to overcome your fear. Share these experiences below.

I felt afraid _____

_____

_____

_____ .

But _____

_____

_____

_____ .

When I was afraid of _____

_____

_____

_____ ,

God _____

_____

_____

_____ .

Now I encourage you to face the fear you're currently experiencing.

MAYBE YOU'RE EXPERIENCING SOME FEARS SURROUNDING THE HOLIDAYS. TODAY, BE VULNERABLE WITH YOURSELF AND WITH GOD ABOUT WHAT IS MAKING YOU FEEL AFRAID.

Example:

I am afraid of *taking a break from social media* .

Because *I'm afraid people won't notice I'm gone and I'll lose touch with my friends* .

I am afraid of _____

_____

Because _____

_____

I am afraid of _____

_____

Because _____

_____

I am afraid of _____

_____

Because _____

_____

I am afraid of _____

_____

Because _____

_____

I am afraid of _____

_____

Because _____

_____

I am afraid of _____

_____

Because _____

_____

I am afraid of _____

_____

Because _____

_____

Take a moment to pray to God,
asking Him to help you acknowledge your fears
and to help you to trust Him to let them go.

_____
_____
_____
_____
_____
_____
_____
_____

Christmas Ornaments

One thing I love about acting is having the opportunity to tell an incredible story. Whether I'm telling the story of a widowed mother of three boys in San Francisco or a mystery-solving librarian from Georgia, stories have defined my life and career for so many years.

Even though I spend lots of my time telling other people's stories, I also love telling the story of my own life. At Christmastime, my story is captured in one special decoration: my Christmas tree! Now I know not everyone collects and cherishes ornaments like I do; maybe your Christmas cards tell your story or a robust collection of Santa figurines or a stack of Christmas books from your childhood take you back to many Christmases ago.

Christmas is a time of storytelling and remembering and cherishing times gone by. When I look at my Christmas ornaments, it takes me back to so many milestones from my kids' lives: "Baby's First Christmas," that homemade ornament from my son's first grade Christmas party that is barely hanging on, a relic from a family vacation gone awry. We have ornaments from ornament exchanges with friends and family that remind me of their steady and faithful presence in my life. These ornaments, some hilarious and gaudy, some tasteful and delicate, are markers of seasons in my life that are long gone—memories of a journey covered in God's faithful fingerprints.

An old hymn, "Blessed Assurance," reads, "This is my story; this is my song. Praising my Savior all the day long." These lyrics remind me of the song my soul sings when I look at my beautiful Christmas tree. My story, my song, is not one that is without cracks and fragmentation and breakage. Just like those old ornaments, there are broken pieces and irreparable damage in my life. But when I look through our ornaments and remember these moments, I'm reminded of God's presence and redeeming work every step of the way. Of the beautiful story He has written and orchestrated since the beginning of time.

This Christmas, think about your own story. Think about the passing of time and the faithful presence of Jesus every step of the way. As you unpack your Christmas decorations and remember the stories that ornaments, figurines, or Christmas cards tell, don't forget the beautiful work of Jesus in your life. Hold that tattered Christmas book in your hands and thank God for the joy that story brought to your now-grown child; place the angel on the top of your Christmas tree and remember the way your dad used to tell you the story of buying that angel from a dingy antique store the night before Christmas. Cherish the memories and stories that make you who you are, and celebrate the faithfulness of God throughout all the years of your life.

King David celebrates God's faithfulness in Psalm 35:27–28, saying, "'The LORD is wonderful! God is glad when all goes well for His servant.' Then I will shout all day, 'Praise the LORD God! He did what was right'" (CEV).

This Christmas, remember the goodness of God. Remember the moments He met you and sustained you. Remember the friends and family He's surrounded you with. The moments He showed up in simple ways like a beautiful rainbow, a gentle snowfall, or a quiet morning curled up in front of your fireplace with a cup of coffee. Remember your story and let it spur you on to joyfully sing God's praises—telling your story to others. And maybe swing by the store and buy an ornament that reminds you of God's constant presence in your life.

The Stars and the Child

by Andrea Hofer Proudfoot

Long, long ago—so long that even the old gray hills have forgotten—the beautiful stars in the sky used to sing together very early every morning, before any of the little people of the world were up. Their songs were made of light and were so clear and strong that the whole heaven would shine when they sang.

One morning, as the stars sang and listened to each other, they heard beautiful music coming swiftly toward them. It was so much louder and sweeter than their own that they all stopped and listened and wondered. It came from far above them, from out the very deepest blue of the sky. It was a new star, and it sang an entirely new song that no one had ever heard before.

"Hark, hark!" the stars cried. "Let us hear what it is saying."

And the beautiful star sang it over and over again, and its song told of a lovely Babe that had come on earth—a Babe so beautiful that it was the joy of the whole world. Yes, so beautiful that when you looked at it you saw real light streaming from its face.

Every little child in the world has light in its face if we but know how to see it, but this little one had so very much that its mother wondered as she looked down upon her lap and saw it there. And there were shepherds there to look at the Babe, and many other people saw it and could not understand.

But the one beautiful star knew—yes, it knew all about it; and what do you think it knew? Why, that this Child was God's own Child and was so good and loving that the whole world when it heard of it would want to know how to be so, too.

This one beautiful star traveled on and on, telling all the way what it knew of the Child, and its light fairly danced through the sky and hung over the very place where the little one lay.

Think about your own story and the many ways God has met you throughout your life. Use these ornaments to draw or write ways that God is writing your story. Think of important moments throughout your life: people, places, or things that God has used to make you who you are!

When Christ was born in Bethlehem,
'Twas night but seemed the noon of day:
The star whose light
Was pure and bright,
Shone with unwav'ring ray;
But one bright star,
One glorious star
Guided the Eastern Magi from afar.

—FROM "WHEN CHRIST
WAS BORN IN BETHLEHEM,"
TRANSLATED FROM THE NEAPOLITAN

Our Shepherd's Heart

Buckle up for today's story—it's wild! A few years back, I got in touch with my "shepherdess" side on a drive down the Malibu coast with my son. We were driving along, minding our own business, when out of nowhere, the truck in front of us hit a bump and the doors swung open. Now, I know it sounds unbelievable, but from the trailer of the truck flew baby goats and sheep! The driver of the truck didn't know its precious cargo was spilling all over the road, so my son and I pulled over and tried to corral the animals. A few other drivers joined us in wrangling the animals, and eventually someone else tracked down the driver of the truck. We gathered all the baby goats and sheep together except one sheep who had escaped. And the driver told me that this one sheep was special; she was older and had just recovered from a surgery.

My son and I got back in the car and went on our way, but I couldn't put that lost sheep out of my mind. It brought me to the parable in Matthew 18 where Jesus says, "If a man owns a hundred sheep, and one of them wanders away, will he not leave the ninety-nine on the hills and go to look for the one that wandered off? And if he finds it, truly I tell you, he is happier about that one sheep than about the ninety-nine that did not wander off. In the same way your Father in heaven is not willing that any of these little ones should perish" (VERSES 12-14 NIV).

It's not often that we so directly and realistically experience a story from the Bible. So much of our world is different now. Most of us rarely encounter sheep outside a petting zoo, and the pursuit of a lost sheep is something few can relate to. But on that fateful day, my eyes were opened to the reality of "the lost sheep" image we often hear about in church sermons.

Jesus is a Savior who cares for the lost sheep. He came to earth so long ago to chase after that sheep. If you are in a season of being lost or alone, if you feel scared or unseen, if you have wandered and can't find your way home, Jesus is for you. He died on the cross for those who have strayed from the safe confines of the Shepherd's watch. He came to earth to pursue us and return us safely to the pasture.

I will forever be grateful for that almost comical moment when we were chasing after baby goats and sheep on a busy road. It gave me such a tangible picture of what it feels like to be loved and pursued by my Savior. Despite so many of my weaknesses and failures—the inconveniences I cause, my disobedience, my wandering, my chasing down other pleasures and masters, my apathetic attitude at times, and my choosing myself over my Savior—Jesus chases me. He is my Good Shepherd, and He came to earth so many years ago as a baby to care for His sheep.

Do you see yourself as His sheep this Christmas season? Do you believe that He wants you enough to leave behind the ninety-nine to pursue you? Do you see the way His life has changed your own by His relentless, overwhelming love for you?

I hope this Christmas you experience this love. I hope you look around for it and let it change the way you live. I hope it gives you confidence to return to your Shepherd who loves you so dearly and chases after you so wildly. I hope you return again and again to the pasture where freedom and joy abound.

The Christmas Rose

by Lizzie Deas (ADAPTED)

When the Magi placed their rich offerings of myrrh, frankincense, and gold by the bed of the sleeping Christ Child, legend says that a shepherd maiden stood outside the door quietly weeping.

She, too, had sought the Christ Child. She, too, desired to bring Him gifts. But she had nothing to offer, for she was very poor indeed. In vain she had searched the countryside over for one little flower to bring Him, but she could find neither bloom nor leaf, for the winter had been cold.

And as she stood there weeping, an angel passing saw her sorrow, and stooping he brushed aside the snow at her feet. And there sprang up on the spot a cluster of beautiful winter roses, waxen white with pink-tipped petals.

"Nor myrrh, nor frankincense, nor gold," said the angel, "is offering more meet for the Christ Child than these pure Christmas Roses."

Joyfully the shepherd maiden gathered the flowers and made her offering to the Holy Child.

Use these pages to reflect on this beautiful psalm about God being your shepherd. Write your name in the blanks throughout the psalm. Then read it aloud, and joyfully and thoughtfully consider the ways God loves and cares for you.

Psalm 23 (NIV)
A psalm of David.

The Lord is _____'s shepherd,

   I [_____] lack nothing.

He makes _____

   lie down in green pastures,

He leads _____ beside quiet waters,

   He refreshes _____'s soul.

He guides _____ along the right paths

   for His name's sake.

Even though I [_____] walk

   through the darkest valley,

I [_____] will fear no evil,

   for You are with _____;

Your rod and Your staff,

   they comfort _____.

You prepare a table before _____

   in the presence of _____'s enemies.

You anoint _____'s head with oil;

   _____'s cup overflows.

Surely Your goodness and love will follow _____

all the days of _____'s life,

and I [_____] will dwell in the house of the

Lord forever.

Take a moment to write down or simply speak out loud a prayer, reflecting on the words you just read in Psalm 23.

_____

_____

_____

_____

_____

_____

_____

_____

O little town of Bethlehem,
How still we see thee lie!
Above thy deep and dreamless sleep
The silent stars go by.
Yet in thy dark streets shineth
The everlasting light;
The hopes and fears of all the years
Are met in thee tonight.
For Christ is born of Mary,
And gathered all above.
While mortals sleep, the angels keep
Their watch of wondering love.
O morning stars, together
Proclaim the holy birth!
And praises sing to God the King
And peace to men on earth.

—FROM "O LITTLE TOWN OF BETHLEHEM"
BY PHILLIPS BROOKS

Unity

I don't know about you, but I sometimes find it hard to focus on joy and maintain a good attitude when the people around me are disagreeing with me or criticizing me for my views. It can be so reassuring to surround yourself with people who think the same way as you! They cheer you on; they support your choices; they make you feel good about your life and where it's headed. It's hard to hear voices that offer criticism or opposing opinions. It can feel frustrating when someone disagrees with you and voices an alternate option.

In many circumstances in our lives we welcome alternate views and value differences in opinion. If a doctor gives you a new diagnosis, most would encourage you to get a second opinion. If you try out a new exercise routine, you'll look for advice on if it's really the most effective. But when it comes to more personal parts of our lives, we often have a difficult time coming to different conclusions. We are not the first generation of people to struggle with this! In Paul's letter to the Ephesian church he writes, "Always be humble and gentle. Patiently put up with each other and love each other. Try your best to let God's Spirit keep your hearts united. Do this by living at peace" (EPHESIANS 4:2-3 CEV).

You'll notice Paul's word choice is very clear. He doesn't instruct believers to agree on everything. He doesn't urge them to avoid conflict completely. He doesn't tell them to correct people when they are wrong and make sure they know what you think. Not at all! Paul encourages these believers to be humble and gentle. He tells them that they will need patience and love to remain unified. It's also important to notice that Paul asks believers to maintain a spirit of *unity*, not uniformity! He doesn't cast judgment on certain believers for worshiping one way or another; instead, he instructs the church to find a bond of peace because of the unity of the Spirit.

These days, you don't have to look far to find people with differing perspectives. Because it's so easy to express your opinions on social media, we often find ourselves surrounded by people who think differently. But what really provides the opportunity to change us is when we listen and respond humbly and lovingly to these opinions. Paul wants believers to "patiently put up with each other," not just walk away when conversations get heated.

You will undoubtedly come into contact with someone who believes something different from you this holiday season. Maybe it's your great-uncle or your cousin's new boyfriend. Maybe you and your kids or your parents have differing views on something. Wherever you find yourself this holiday, remember the common bond we share: the need for a Savior! We share in our absolute inability to live a holy life and our complete dependence on a God who sent His Son. We share the message of hope and grace that the Gospel provides. We share the need for humility because we are fallen, broken people.

As you share stories, thoughts, and opinions throughout the Advent season, remind yourself why Jesus came to earth. He lived a life of humility, bearing with sinful people and allowing them to misrepresent, mock, and manipulate His words and actions. Jesus never turned on these people; instead, He died for them. He lived a life that Paul calls us to live and provided the ultimate opportunity for us to unify under a common need: the need for Him in our lives!

Mama's Happy Christmas

by Miriam T. Barnard

It had seemed to the little Wendell children that they would have a very sad Christmas. Mama had been very ill, and Papa had been so anxious about Mama that he could not think of anything else.

When Christmas Day came, however, Mama was so much better that she could lie on the lounge. The children all brought their stockings into her room to open them.

"You children all seem as happy as if you had had your usual Christmas tree," said Mama, as they sat around her.

"Why, I *never* had such a happy Christmas before," said sweet little Agnes. "And it's just because you are well again."

"Now I think you must all run out for the rest of the day," said the nurse, "because your mama wants to see you all again this evening."

"I wish we could do something expressly for Mama's amusement," said Agnes, when they had gone into the nursery.

"How would you like to have some tableaux in here?" asked their French governess, Miss Marcelle.

"Oh, yes," they all cried. "It would be fun! Mama loves tableaux."

So, all day long they were busy arranging five tableaux for the evening. The tableaux were to be in the room that had folding doors opening into Mama's sitting room.

At the proper time, Miss Marcelle stepped outside the folding doors and made a pretty little speech. She said that some young ladies and a young gentleman had asked permission to show some tableaux to Mrs. Wendell if she would like to see them. Mrs. Wendell replied that she would be charmed.

Then mademoiselle announced the tableaux, opening the doors wide for each one. This is a list of the tableaux: First, *The Sleeping Beauty*; second, *Little Red Riding Hood*; third, *The Fairy Queen*; fourth, *Old Mother Hubbard*; fifth, *The Lord High Admiral*.

Miss Marcelle had arranged everything so nicely, and Celeste, the French maid, helped so much with the dressing that the pictures all went off without a single mistake.

Mama was delighted. She said she must kiss those dear young ladies and that delightful young man who had given her such a charming surprise.

So, all the children came in rosy and smiling.

"Didn't you know us?" asked the little Lord Admiral.

"I know this," said Mama. "I am like Agnes. I *never* had such a happy Christmas before."

The Bible regularly reminds followers of Jesus to have a spirit of unity. Unity brings the peace and joy we want in our lives—especially during the Christmas season. Look at the heart below. In each piece of the broken heart, write one thing that tends to divide people.

THE BEAUTY OF LIFE WITH JESUS IS THAT WE ARE ALL UNITED AROUND ONE THING:
the cross!

Inside the cross, write down the ways that we can love others who are different from us as a reminder that God calls us to a life of unity.

Clothe Yourself

Holidays always seem to magnify the feeling of love. Something about the giving and the celebrating fills me to the brim with love for the people in my life. But occasionally that bubbly, giddy feeling of love is nowhere to be found, and I find myself riddled with angst. There's disappointment with a loved one who bailed on me, irritation at the constant comparison game with my good-at-everything friend, or a short temper with a family member. It's not the holiday spirit I'm accustomed to, but I've been around long enough to know that these unsettling feelings are a real part of the holidays for most of us.

In those moments, I have to ask myself, "How would Jesus respond to this person?" and really stop to consider my next move. I've been so challenged by the passage in Colossians 3 that describes the life and action of "God's chosen people" (VERSE 12 NIV). Paul, the author of Colossians, wrote, "Clothe yourselves with compassion, kindness, humility, gentleness and patience. Bear with each other and forgive one another if any of you has a grievance against someone. Forgive as the Lord forgave you" (VERSES 12-13 NIV).

Those words bring me back to my knees, asking for the strength and willingness to joyfully and compassionately love people who leave me feeling frustrated or misunderstood. I have to ask, *What am I clothing myself with today?*

Am I committed to putting on gentleness? Do I let that gentleness fuel me when I find myself frustrated with my husband? Do I put on patience each morning? Does this patience change the way I speak to my kids or family members? Am I a friend who "bears with" my friends? Do I share in their grief or send a cursory text of comfort? Do I practice celebrating my friends in their moments of great joy, or do I focus on comparing myself to them to build my own ego? Am I quick to forgive people who wrong me, or do I store away people's wrongdoings and use it against them in the future? These occurrences are nothing special, but each presents an opportunity to depend more fully on Jesus for a spirit of love.

Let's allow these words from Paul to move us to action this Christmas. As we go about our days, we will inevitably run into people and circumstances that stir up frustration, insecurity, or bitterness. It's inescapable! It leaves us with a choice: Will we respond in Christlikeness or human-likeness? Will we tap into that supernatural Spirit-filled love or rely on our own weak selves to work through hard moments?

Christmas is ultimately about the incredible, sacrificial, uncomfortable love that Jesus demonstrated by leaving His Father's side and entering into our broken and fallen world. He demonstrated Colossians 3 by clothing Himself in compassion, despite being mocked; humility, despite living a perfect life; gentleness and patience, despite people beating and berating Him. Jesus came to earth to bear with us—to experience the daily challenges and temptations of life so that we were not alone in our pursuit of holiness. Jesus forgave us and demonstrated this forgiveness by selflessly dying on the cross for us.

This Christmas, remember that you serve a Savior who loves you with compassion, humility, gentleness, and patience. He bears with you. He forgives you. Enjoy the sweetness and freedom that this love brings you—and then extend it to others. Allow love to be more than a temporary feeling of excitement. Let's demonstrate the love modeled for us by Jesus: a deep, sacrificial, grace-filled, transformative love.

The Wooden Shoes of Little Wolff

by François Coppée (ADAPTED)

Long ago in a city of the North of Europe there was a little boy, just seven years old, whose name was Wolff. He was an orphan and lived with his aunt, a hard-hearted, avaricious old woman, who never kissed him but once a year, on New Year's Day, and who sighed with regret every time she gave him a bowlful of soup. Wolff was so sweet-tempered that he loved the old woman in spite of her bad treatment.

As Wolff's aunt was known to have a house of her own and a woolen stocking full of gold, she did not dare to send her nephew to the school for the poor. But she wrangled so that the schoolmaster of the rich boys' school was forced to lower his price and admit little Wolff among his pupils. The bad schoolmaster was vexed to have a boy so meanly clad and who paid so little, and he punished little Wolff severely without cause. Wolff's comrades, the sons of rich citizens, mocked him relentlessly.

On Christmas Eve, the schoolmaster took his pupils to midnight mass. The other boys donned fur-lined caps, padded jackets, gloves and knitted mittens, and strong shoes with thick soles. Wolff shivered in his thin everyday clothes, socks, and wooden shoes.

The boys boasted of the midnight treats awaiting them at home and talked about what the Christ Child would leave in their shoes by the fire after they went to bed. Wolff knew his miserly aunt would send him to bed without any supper, but as he had been good and industrious all year, he trusted that the Christ Child would not forget him, so he meant that night to set his wooden shoes on the hearth.

The midnight mass was ended. The worshipers hurried away. But under the porch, seated on a stone bench, was a child asleep—a little child dressed in a white garment with bare feet exposed to the cold. He was not a beggar, for his dress was clean and new, and beside him upon the ground, tied in a cloth, were the tools of a carpenter's apprentice.

The pupils passed with indifference before the unknown child. Some, the sons of the greatest men in the city, cast looks of scorn on the barefooted one. But little Wolff stopped, deeply moved before the beautiful, sleeping child.

"How dreadful!" said the orphan to himself. "This poor little one goes without stockings in weather so cold! And he has no shoe to leave beside him while he sleeps, so that the Christ Child may place something in it to comfort him."

Carried away by his tender heart, Wolff removed the wooden shoe from his right foot and placed it before the sleeping child, and as best as he was able, he hopped and limped through the snow and returned to his aunt.

"You good-for-nothing!" cried the old woman, full of rage when she saw one of his shoes missing. "What have you done with your shoe, little beggar? I will place the other shoe in the fireplace, and tonight the Christ Child will put in a rod to whip you when you wake! Tomorrow you shall have nothing to eat but water and dry bread."

But in the morning the fireplace was filled with bright toys, boxes of sugarplums, and riches of all sorts. Incredibly, the wooden shoe that Wolff had given to the vagabond was standing beside the other shoe, and it was full of treasures.

The children of the rich men, whose parents wished to surprise them with the most beautiful gifts, had found nothing but switches in their shoes!

Then all the people knew that the beautiful, sleeping child, beside whom had lain the carpenter's tools, was the Christ Child Himself, and that He had rewarded the faith and charity of little Wolff.

Look through the following words that God asks us to clothe ourselves in: compassion, kindness, humility, quiet strength, discipline, forgiveness, contentment, even-temperament, love. Think about situations you will encounter this Christmas. What do you need to clothe yourself in as you head into this holiday season?

CHRISTMAS SITUATIONS	CLOTHE YOURSELF
	□ compassion □ kindness □ humility □ quiet strength □ discipline □ forgiveness □ contentment □ love □ even-temperament
	□ compassion □ kindness □ humility □ quiet strength □ discipline □ forgiveness □ contentment □ love □ even-temperament
	□ compassion □ kindness □ humility □ quiet strength □ discipline □ forgiveness □ contentment □ love □ even-temperament
	□ compassion □ kindness □ humility □ quiet strength □ discipline □ forgiveness □ contentment □ love □ even-temperament
	□ compassion □ kindness □ humility □ quiet strength □ discipline □ forgiveness □ contentment □ love □ even-temperament
	□ compassion □ kindness □ humility □ quiet strength □ discipline □ forgiveness □ contentment □ love □ even-temperament

O come, all ye faithful,
Joyful and triumphant!
O come ye, O come ye to Bethlehem;
Come and behold Him
Born the King of Angels:
O come, let us adore Him . . . .
Yea, Lord, we greet thee,
Born this happy morning;
Jesus, to Thee be glory given!
Word of the Father,
Now in flesh appearing!
O come, let us adore Him.

—FROM "O COME, ALL YE FAITHFUL"
BY FREDERICK OAKELEY

Planting and Reaping

Have you ever picked vegetables from a garden? Wandered through the new growth and discovered a juicy, ripe tomato or a perfectly green pepper? Have you ever bit into a fresh cucumber or enjoyed basil—*straight from the garden*? This is seriously one of my favorite ways to enjoy food. It's. So. Good. I love the experience of watching the whole journey from tiny seed to a delicious meal. It's food with a story, and who doesn't love a good story. Right? Food that I waited for and hoped for. This may sound a little crazy, but there's something unspeakably *profound* about this process.

I often wonder if the examples in the Bible about sowing seeds and reaping a harvest would've hit home more in Bible times. They must've been so familiar with the tedious and grueling work of planting seeds and tending to them for months and months before enjoying the fruit (or veggie) of their labors. Jesus uses this language throughout the New Testament in parables, and Paul echoes this analogy in his second letter to the Corinthians: "Remember this—a farmer who plants only a few seeds will get a small crop. But the one who plants generously will get a generous crop" (II CORINTHIANS 9:6 NLT). These words are so straightforward and direct, and yet I find them difficult to carry out.

Christmas is a season where we really do reap. We feel the efforts of our financial endeavors, relational pursuits, and spiritual investments. So this Christmastime think back on the planting you did this year. Did you plant generously? Did you give everything you had and stay in step with the ways God asked you to give? Or was it a year of planting sparingly? Did it feel difficult to give and give and give more? We all have different seasons of life where giving comes more naturally. But in seasons where it is difficult, it helps to remember what purpose it serves. Paul reminds the church in Corinth to plant generously because it allows for a plentiful harvest! It provides joy for the giver and the receiver. It creates a God-honoring dynamic of openhandedness and generosity. It imitates Jesus' heart in giving all that He had for the benefit of others.

As we lean into waiting during this Christmas season, remind yourself of the incredible joy that comes with a generous reaping. The process of growing and harvesting is slow. There are so many moments where we see no progress, no promise of goodness to come, and we must wait patiently for growth. As we plant seeds in our own lives, we often feel a similar stalemate. That relationship feels stalled out, the financial sacrifices go unnoticed, the time spent with Jesus in the morning isn't stopping us from getting angry at night. We grow frustrated as the patterns in our lives don't change. But please hear me. I know the waiting is hard. It's hard for me, too. But God promises to meet us in our planting. He provides the light, water, and protection that are needed for growth. We are not promised to get exactly what we want or to avoid moments of suffering. But we are promised a generous reaping when we plant generously. God's generosity provides us peace, security, confidence, eternal satisfaction, and joy. When we plant in God's name, we reap the benefits of a lasting, satisfying relationship with Him.

As much as I love to bite into a magnificent, freshly picked tomato, I know there is nothing that will taste as sweet as investing in God's kingdom. This Christmastime, open your eyes to the spaces and chances you have to plant seeds. Where can you give of your gifts and time that will reap eternal rewards?

A Christmas Legend

by Florence Scannell

As the story goes, it was Christmas Eve. The night was very dark and the snow falling fast, as Hermann, the charcoal burner, drew his cloak tighter around him. The wind whistled fiercely through the trees of the Black Forest. He had been to carry a load to a castle near and was now hastening home to his little hut. Although he worked very hard, he was poor, gaining barely enough for the wants of his wife and four little children. He was thinking of them when he heard a faint wailing. Guided by the sound, he groped about and found a little child, scantily clothed, shivering and sobbing by himself in the snow.

"Why, little one, have they left you here all alone to face this cruel blast?"

The child answered nothing but looked piteously up in the charcoal burner's face.

"Well, I cannot leave you here. You would be dead before the morning."

So Hermann raised the child in his arms, wrapping the child in his cloak and warming his little cold hands in his bosom. When he arrived at his hut, he put down the child and tapped at the door, which was immediately thrown open, and the children rushed to meet him.

"Here, wife, is a guest to our Christmas Eve supper," said he, leading in the little one, who held timidly to his finger with his tiny hand.

"And welcome he is," said the wife. "Now let him come and warm himself by the fire."

The children all pressed round to welcome and gaze at the little newcomer. They showed him their pretty fir tree, decorated with bright, colored lamps in honor of Christmas Eve, which the good mother had endeavored to make a fete for the children.

Then they sat down to supper, each child contributing of its portion for the guest, looking with admiration at his clear, blue eyes and golden hair, which shone so as to shed a brighter light in the little room. And as they gazed, it grew into a sort of halo round his head, and his eyes beamed with a heavenly luster. Soon two white wings appeared at his shoulders, and he seemed to grow larger and larger. Then the beautiful vision vanished, spreading out his hands as in benediction over them.

Hermann and his wife fell on their knees, exclaiming in awestruck voices, "The holy Christ Child!" and then embraced their wondering children in joy and thankfulness that they had entertained the heavenly Guest.

The next morning, as Hermann passed by the place where he had found the fair child, he saw a cluster of lovely white flowers with dark green leaves, looking as though the snow itself had blossomed. Hermann plucked some and carried them reverently home to his wife and children, who treasured the fair blossoms and tended them carefully in remembrance of that wonderful Christmas Eve. They call the flowers Chrysanthemums, and every year, as the time came round, they put aside a portion of their feast and gave it to some poor little child, according to the words of the Christ: "Inasmuch as ye have done it unto one of the least of these my brethren, ye have done it unto me" (MATTHEW 25:40 KJV).

Consider the growth in your own life.

What areas are ready to harvest? You've invested in it, watched it grow, and now it's really producing fruit. Label the plants in full bloom with these areas and write what you enjoy about the harvest. Celebrate all that God has done in these areas of your life!

Example: Taking the time to read my Bible every morning.
I'm enjoying hearing Scripture in my mind throughout the day.
It has brought me so much joy and peace.

_____   _____

_____   _____

_____   _____

_____   _____

What areas are still in process? The growth has maybe stalled out or is having a hard time getting to a full, rich place. What do you need to do to help these areas grow? Label the plants in process and write down steps you'll take to help them flourish.

Example: I want to develop a rich prayer life, but I never make time for it. I want to start every morning by praying.

Are there areas in your life that are still in the seed stage? Which of these areas do you hope to plant this year? How will you get started, and what do you hope comes from it?

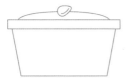 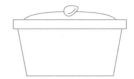

Example: I want to start talking with my friend about Jesus.
I'm going to schedule coffee with her to connect more regularly.

_____

_____

_____

_____

Hark! the herald angels sing,
"Glory to the newborn King:
Peace on earth, and mercy mild,
God and sinners reconcil'd!"
Joyful, all ye nations, rise,
Join the triumph of the skies.
With the angelic host proclaim,
"Christ is born in Bethlehem."
Hark! the herald angels sing,
"Glory to the newborn King!"

—FROM "HARK! THE HERALD ANGELS SING"
BY CHARLES WESLEY

Comparison

In a season so consumed with hosting and decorating and purchasing, there's an inevitable tendency to be consumed by the comparison game. It's easy, after all, to feel sheepish that your holiday decorations are store-bought when your neighbor's home is covered in homemade garlands, snowflakes, and hand-lettered signage. You might cringe when you realize you'll have to wear the same dress to the holiday work party because a new dress just isn't in the budget this year. And oh, the agony of choosing an appetizer for the family potluck knowing you'll be outdone again by your sister's Food Network–worthy masterpiece. Christmastime can easily prey on our insecurities, reminding us of the things or relationships or skills we wish we had.

Isn't this such a shame? When we read on paper the traps we so easily fall into, it's obvious that comparison will only hurt us this Christmas season. But nevertheless, we find ourselves scrolling our feeds feeling less and less confident in our ability to create a meaningful Christmas experience for our friends and families. We believe the lie that we need more money, better relationships, more gifts, and more beautiful decorations to truly find joy in the holiday season.

This lie permeates our society in such a deep way. But the Bible tells us that our worth is found not in what we do or what we have but in *who God says we are*. He doesn't compare us to other people. In His eyes, we are all worthy of His love. God loves us so much that He sent His Son, Jesus, to free us from all the things that keep us from having a real relationship with God—things like pride, selfishness, hatred, unforgiveness, and unkindness. It's easy to attempt to fix comparison by finding out what really makes you special or unique—by deciding to be known for incredible gift-giving skills or mastering the Christmas cookie; to find your identity in serving at your church or giving to the poor. None of these pursuits are bad; there is an incredible number of ways to use the giftings that God blessed you with, but the reality is, comparison is more quickly addressed by realizing the need we *all* have for a Savior.

You may be naturally gifted in many areas or feel completely inept in all things Christmas, and the reality is that Jesus died for you. Your worth is not measured by the things you do or accomplish. Identity cannot be established based on good deeds or kind words. You have value because you were created specifically and purposefully by God. You have lived a life that is marked by sin and failure, and yet Jesus died for you! I say this not to discourage you from cultivating loving behavior or skills that bless others but to free you from the pursuit of being loved for what you do.

Paul reminds us in Romans that "all have sinned and fall short of the glory of God" (3:23 NIV). At Christmas, we celebrate the birth of Jesus, of God with us. We celebrate and lift up His glory above our own. It's this reality that frees us from the comparison game. We are created by a God who loves us and died for us in spite of our sin. His love extends to us in our darkest moments and in the moments where we truly shine.

This Christmas, look at your own life. Don't be distracted by the lives of those around you. Do your life and your home and your extracurriculars bring glory to God? Do they point to His creativity in making you and His goodness in saving you? Don't be distracted by the temptation to compare yourself to others or to feel like you have little or nothing to offer. Instead, embrace the freedom of living only for God.

Often the cure for comparison is to remember two things: First, we have all sinned and all fall short of God's glory. And second, you were created magnificently by a God who loves you!

The Legend of the "White Gifts"

by *Phebe A. Curtiss* (ADAPTED)

A great many years ago in a land far away from us there was a certain king who was dearly beloved by all his people. Men admired him because he was strong and just. Women trusted him because he was pure and true, and the children loved him because of his gentleness and tenderness toward them. He was never so burdened with affairs of state that he could not stop to speak a pleasant word of greeting to the tiniest child, and the very poorest of his subjects knew they could count upon his interest in them.

This deep-seated love and reverence for their king made the people of this country wish for a way to give expression to it so that he would understand it. Many consultations were held and one after another the plans suggested were rejected, but at last a most happy solution was found.

They decided that on the king's birthday the people should all bring him gifts, but they wanted in some way to let him know that these gifts were the expression of a love on the part of the giver that was pure and true and unselfish, and in order to show that, it was decided that each gift should be a "White Gift."

The king heard about this beautiful plan, and it touched his heart in a wonderful way. You can just imagine the excitement there was all over the land as the king's birthday drew near. All sorts of loving sacrifices had been made, and everyone was anxious to make his gift the very best he had to offer.

At last the day dawned, and eagerly the people came dressed in white and carrying their gifts. To their surprise they were ushered into a great big room—the largest one in the palace. They stood in silence when they first entered it, for it was beautiful beyond all expression—the floor was white marble; the ceiling looked like a mass of soft, white fluffy clouds; the walls were hung with beautiful white silken draperies; and all the furnishings were white. In one end of the room stood a stately white throne, and seated upon it was their beloved ruler. He was clad in shining white robes, and his attendants—all dressed in white—were grouped around him.

Then came the presentation of the gifts. In those days it was just as it is now—there were many people who had great wealth, and they brought gifts that were generous in proportion to their wealth. One brought a handful of pearls, another a number of carved ivories. There were beautiful laces and silks and embroideries, all in pure white, and even splendid white chargers were brought to his majesty.

But many of the people were poor—some of them very poor. Some of the women brought handfuls of white rice, some of the boys brought their favorite white pigeons, and one dear little girl smilingly gave him a pure white rose.

It was wonderful to watch the king as each one came and kneeled before him as he presented his gift. He never seemed to notice whether the gift was great or small; he regarded not one gift above another so long as all were white. Never had the king been so happy as he was that day and never had such real joy filled the hearts of the people. And so it came to pass that year after year on the king's birthday the people came from here and there and everywhere and brought gifts that showed that their love was pure, strong, true, and without stain. And year after year the king regarded not one gift above another.

Take time to think through each of the following verses from Psalm 139. Write down your responses to how the words communicate God's love for you.

> You have searched me, LORD,
>   and You know me.
> You know when I sit and when I rise;
>   You perceive my thoughts from afar.
> You discern my going out and my lying down;
>   You are familiar with all my ways.

PSALM 139:1-3 (NIV)

.

_____

_____

_____

_____

_____

_____

_____

_____

_____

_____

_____

Where can I go from Your Spirit?
   Where can I flee from Your presence?
If I go up to the heavens, You are there;
   if I make my bed in the depths, You are there.
If I rise on the wings of the dawn,
   if I settle on the far side of the sea,
even there Your hand will guide me,
   Your right hand will hold me fast.

PSALM 139:7–10 (NIV)

For You created my inmost being;
   You knit me together in my mother's womb.
I praise You because I am fearfully and wonderfully made;
   Your works are wonderful,
   I know that full well.
My frame was not hidden from You
   when I was made in the secret place,
   when I was woven together in the depths of the earth.
Your eyes saw my unformed body;
   all the days ordained for me were written in Your book
   before one of them came to be.

PSALM 139:13-16 (NIV)

The first Noel, the angels say
To Bethlehem's shepherds as they lay.
At midnight watch, when keeping sheep,
The winter wild, the light snow deep.
Noel, Noel, Noel, Noel
Born is the King of Israel.
The shepherds rose, and saw a star
Bright in the East, beyond them far,
Its beauty gave them great delight,
This star it set now day nor night.
Noel, Noel, Noel, Noel
Born is the King of Israel.

—FROM "THE FIRST NOEL"
(AUTHOR UNKNOWN)

Honoring God

If you interact with me at all on social media, you know I love food and exercise! I love to cook, grow vegetables in my garden, work with my amazing trainer, and spend quality time loving and caring for my body. I think that caring well for the bodies God gave us is crucial to enjoying life here on earth!

In Paul's letter to the Corinthians, he writes, "You surely know that your body is a temple where the Holy Spirit lives. The Spirit is in you and is a gift from God. You are no longer your own. God paid a great price for you. So use your body to honor God" (I CORINTHIANS 6:19-20 CEV). Christmastime can often be a season where we struggle to honor God with our bodies—with the things we do, the activities we prioritize, the people we hang out with. So often our schedules are demanding and we lack rest, sleep, and regular exercise. We attend multiple parties and gatherings that are full of tempting food. Now, I'm not saying we shouldn't eat yummy food at Christmastime. That's not the point here. But these words from Paul give us helpful instruction for caring for our earthly bodies in tandem with our heavenly bodies.

You'll notice that the Bible never offers a weekly workout routine or "the best breakfasts for losing weight" or even commentary on right and wrong in this realm. Instead God gave us the Holy Spirit to help navigate what it looks like to honor God with our bodies. How often do we stop to consider how God sees us? Psalm 139 reminds us that we are "knit . . . together" and "fearfully and wonderfully made" (VERSES 13-14 NIV). Our bodies were made with purpose and intention. They were knit together with meticulous detail and care. Our bodies show up for us on a daily basis and so often do what we need them to do: survive sleepless nights with a newborn baby, work long hours on our feet at a job, fight debilitating diseases. Our bodies not only survive difficult seasons but also do so much that we don't take the time to notice or admire. Our hearts beat. Our lungs fill. Our brains signal us to stop and notice and enjoy. These are bodies that God has given us, and we honor Him when we take care of what He has created.

Our bodies were made by a creative and loving God and given to us to treasure and care for while on earth. But what does that mean this Christmas season? The beauty of Paul's instruction in Corinthians is that *honor* looks different for different people. Perhaps this Christmas season, honoring God with your body means saying no to hosting the big Christmas party or catering the meal instead of staying up for countless nights slaving away in the kitchen. Maybe honoring God with your body means enjoying a delicious Christmas cookie for breakfast with your sweet toddler. Maybe honoring God with your body means turning off the Christmas movie and enjoying a walk with your spouse.

Part of honoring God with your body includes viewing your body as a "temple." A temple is a place for worship and a dwelling place of God. Is your body being used to further God's kingdom and worship Him? Do the words from your mouth worship Him? Do the works of your hands help build His kingdom? Do your feet carry you to places of loving and serving God's children? Do you have the courage to say no to good things so you allow yourself the time to do what you know is *best*? I know this last one can be a tough one.

Christmas is a time to enjoy the goodness of our Creator. To praise Him that we are so fearfully and wonderfully made. To set aside time each day to honor Him by caring for the bodies He gave us. To prioritize the things that *really* matter. Don't buy into the world's message about our bodies! You were made beautifully by a Creator who treasures you from your head to your toes.

The Promise

by Maud Lindsay

There was once a harper who played such beautiful music and sang such beautiful songs that his fame spread throughout the whole land. At last the king heard of him and sent messengers to bring him to the palace.

"I will neither eat nor sleep till I have seen your face and heard the sound of your harp." This was the message the king sent to the harper.

When the king's messengers reached the harper's house they called, "Hail, harper! Come out and listen, for we have something to tell you that will make you glad."

But when the harper heard the king's message, he was sad, for he had a wife and a child and a little brown dog, and he was sorry to leave them and they were sorry to have him go. "Stay with us," they begged.

But the harper said, "I *must* go, for it would be discourtesy to disappoint the king. But as sure as holly berries are red and pine is green, I will come back by Christmas Day to eat my share of the Christmas pudding and sing the Christmas songs by my own fireside." And when he had promised this, he hung his harp upon his back and went away with the messengers to the king's palace.

The king welcomed him with joy, and many things were done in his honor. He slept on a bed of softest down and ate from a plate of gold at the king's own table. And when he sang, everybody and everything, from the king himself to the mouse in the palace pantry, stood still to listen.

No matter what he was doing, however, he never forgot the promise that he had made to his wife and his child and his little brown dog, and when the day before Christmas came, he took his harp in his hand and went to tell the king goodbye.

Now the king was loath to have the harper leave him, and he said to him, "I will give you a horse if you will stay to play and sing before my throne on Christmas Day."

But the harper answered, "I cannot stay, for I have a wife and a child and a little brown dog, and I have promised them to be at home by Christmas Day."

Then the king said, "If you will stay to play and sing before my throne on Christmas Day, I will give to you a wonderful tree that summer or winter is never bare, and silver and gold will fall for you whenever you shake this little tree."

But the harper said, "I must not stay."

Then the king said, "If you will stay on Christmas Day, one tune to play and one song to sing, I will give you a velvet robe to wear, and you may sit beside me here with a ring on your finger and a crown on your head."

But the harper answered, "I will not stay." He wrapped his old cloak about him, and hung his harp upon his back, and went out from the king's palace without another word.

He had not gone far when it started to snow. The paths were all hidden, and the harper stumbled and fell, but he would not turn back. The snow froze on the ground and the harper's breath froze in the air. He shivered and shook, but he would not turn back.

On he went till the last glimmer of daylight faded. "If I cannot see, I can sing," said he, and he sang in the forest joyously. The snow ceased its falling, and as he sang, the darkness turned to wondrous light, and close at hand the harper saw the open doorway of his home.

The wife and the child and the little brown dog were watching and waiting, and they welcomed the harper with great joy. The holly berries were red in the Christmas wreaths; their Christmas tree was a young green pine; the Christmas pudding was full of plums; and the harper was happier than a king as he sat by his own fireside to sing.

HOW DO YOU HONOR GOD
WITH YOUR BODY? HOW CAN YOU
CELEBRATE ALL THE DIFFERENT PARTS
OF YOURSELF THAT GOD MADE
AND WANTS TO USE?

In each section, draw and caption the ways you can honor
God and celebrate that part.

Body

Exercise

Dark Chocolate

Mind

Reading a good book

Heart

*Make time for coffee
with good friends
who make me feel loved*

Soul

Memorize Scripture

Angels from the realms of glory
Wing your flight o'er all the earth!
Ye who sang Creation's story,
Now proclaim Messiah's birth!
Come and worship, come and worship,
Worship Christ, the newborn King.

—FROM "ANGELS FROM
THE REALMS OF GLORY"
BY JAMES MONTGOMERY

Life to the Full

I adore everything about Christmas. It's a time of celebration. And who doesn't love to celebrate? Parties, festive Christmas cards, spending time and money on gifts for people you love—it's a season that brings so much joy. But sometimes we let the celebration unfold without connecting it to the deeper reason for our joy at Christmastime. We forget that faith in a good, faithful God through a relationship with Jesus is what ultimately causes us to celebrate.

Sometimes it's easy to let faith become an obligation or duty rather than a celebration of what Jesus did for us on the cross. The joy and freedom get lost under a pile of "shoulds" and "coulds" and steal the beauty of life with Christ. There is something so incredible about joining the reality of what Jesus did on the cross with the festivities at Christmastime. It undergirds all our natural joy with a deep, satisfying reason to celebrate.

It's so crucial to see joy as something God encourages. Let the things that bring you joy in your life spill over into encounters with a Savior who wants you to experience goodness in even the simplest pleasures. This Christmas, look outside your window and marvel at the creative God who formed each tree, each magical snowflake. Sit and drink a cup of hot chocolate and celebrate the miracle of life. Laugh your head off during a game of charades with friends and revel in the love you share with them. Cozy up with a good book and thank God for the power of words.

God is in each moment of your day; He provides richness and goodness and abundance in the small things and big things. In the book of John, Jesus tells a parable about the Good Shepherd—who is Jesus Himself. He ends the parable by explaining that He came so that we (His sheep) "may have life, and have it to the full" (JOHN 10:10 NIV).

This is the reason we celebrate Christmas. Jesus came! He didn't just come to save us and leave us with a life of obligation and duty. He died on the cross for us that we might live in the freedom of His death and live a life full of abundance.

Abundant life does not guarantee us freedom from pain or suffering. It doesn't mean life will be easy every day or that we will never be affected by the consequences of sin. But abundant life does guarantee that we have access to contentment, satisfaction, joy, and love, which come through Christ.

This Christmas season, remind yourself of the rich, beautiful life you have access to because of God's love for you. See each moment this Christmas as a reason to celebrate a good Savior who came to earth so many years ago to rescue and satisfy your soul.

Look around you and make this season one of true joy! Start by noticing the small pleasures that God offers us: delicious food, incredible sunsets, a beautifully wrapped gift. But then take a look at the deeper narrative we all have access to: joy and satisfaction in the midst of difficult circumstances, tender moments with a loved one who is ill, simple experiences in place of gifts during a time of financial difficulty, freedom from a life of "shoulds" and "coulds" because of the gift of salvation. You are loved by a God who offers life to the full. Don't miss the chance to celebrate your Savior this December!

Christmas

by J. E. Pauley

The days speed by, and thus the year,
The world awakes, finds Christmas here;
The day is welcomed with good cheer
Through every land, both far and near,
  Where Christ is not rejected.

These days by thousands have passed by
Since to the wise men's watchful eye
The star appeared, 'twas shining high,
And lighted up the Eastern sky,
  As prophets had expected.

They quickly sought that humble place,
That they might see that infant's face,
And praise Him Savior of our race,
A token of God's loving grace,
  And saving plan perfected.

Though now from earth He's far away,
His grace is here, and sure we may
Give praise to Him, as well as they
Who sought him on His first birthday
  With presents they'd selected.

His grace sufficient is to bring
Us, at death, to where He's King,
Where angels make all heaven ring
On Christmas Day, with songs they sing.
  If by us He's accepted.

Use these lists to brainstorm the many joys, big and small, that you see around you. Think of all the ways that you can enjoy the fullness of life with Christ!

I SEE GOD'S JOY IN MY HOME THROUGH

❋ _____   ❋ _____

❋ _____   ❋ _____

❋ _____   ❋ _____

❋ _____   ❋ _____

I SEE GOD'S JOY IN THE WORLD THROUGH

❋ _____   ❋ _____

❋ _____   ❋ _____

❋ _____   ❋ _____

❋ _____   ❋ _____

I SEE GOD'S JOY IN MY FAMILY THROUGH:

❄ _____   ❄ _____

❄ _____   ❄ _____

❄ _____   ❄ _____

❄ _____   ❄ _____

I SEE GOD'S JOY IN MY WORK THROUGH:

❄ _____   ❄ _____

❄ _____   ❄ _____

❄ _____   ❄ _____

❄ _____   ❄ _____

I SEE GOD'S JOY IN MY FRIENDS THROUGH:

❄ _____   ❄ _____

❄ _____   ❄ _____

❄ _____   ❄ _____

❄ _____   ❄ _____

I SEE GOD'S JOY IN
DIFFICULT CIRCUMSTANCES THROUGH:

❄ _____   ❄ _____

❄ _____   ❄ _____

❄ _____   ❄ _____

❄ _____   ❄ _____

Seek Jesus

Have you ever gone on a binge of online shopping trying to find the perfect gift? I love online shopping. I love that I don't have to leave my house and that I can sit, cozy on my couch, and find the perfect gifts for my friends and family. But it's a big world of endless shopping out there. It's easy to get lost in the hunt for that perfect shirt with a unique but cute pair of earrings that match just right with the cute scarf that you found on sale. I think you catch my drift.

I've found myself at the end of a long session of hunting for great gifts online feeling exhausted by my pursuit. And it begs the question, How often do I seek after God in that same way? To the point of exhaustion? For most of us, this is not the reality in our lives. Most often we meet with our heavenly Father when it feels convenient or necessary. Does your heart long for Him the way it longs for a great new purse under your Christmas tree? Does it chase after His Word and truth the way it chases after the reservation at the new restaurant in town? Do you push yourself to make time for Him the way you make time for a good workout?

These questions are challenging because so often our priorities get out of whack. We go after things that are lovely and wonderful but not crucial to our souls! The beauty of life with God, though, is that finding Him is not as difficult as some of our other pursuits. Matthew 7:7 reminds us that if we seek Him, we *will* find Him.

But how do we find Him? The beautiful truth about the Lord is that He is everywhere. You might encounter His creativity when you look down at your baby boy's wispy eyelashes or witness His compassion after receiving a needed hug from a friend. His goodness might surprise you in an unplanned exchange at the grocery store. You might read a challenging truth in Scripture that points you back to life to the full instead of life as we want it. God is in your church, your home, your Bible. He is waiting and willing to know you and meet you and spend time with you.

This Christmas season, make time to seek after God. Time and time again in Scripture, we see that those who seek after God's wisdom, truth, and love do not return void. He meets the weak, the weary, the lonely, the doubters, the self-righteous, the sick, the fearful, and He gives them strength, endurance, assurance, and courage. Chasing after your heavenly Father is not a pursuit that will leave you feeling empty and alone. You won't be let down. You won't be disappointed. His goodness is better than any Christmas sale, any perfect pair of shoes, any surprise gift you could find online.

This Christmas season, make space in your life to pursue the Lord. Ask Him to meet you, to encourage you, to challenge you, to make you more like Him. Ask Him to refresh you with His words of truth and grace. Ask Him to direct you in your moments of uncertainty or doubt. Ask Him to focus your attention on what matters most this Christmas season. For each of us, God directs our paths differently. Seek what God has for you this month and know with great confidence that this pursuit will leave you full of joy and satisfaction!

The Gift of the Magi

by O. Henry (ADAPTED)

Three times Della counted her money. One dollar and eighty-seven cents. And the next day would be Christmas. Della flopped down on the shabby little couch and howled. Soon Mr. James Dillingham Young would arrive home. He was called "Jim" by Mrs. James Dillingham Young, also known as Della.

She had been saving every penny she could for months. She had spent hours planning to buy something nice for him—something worthy to be owned by Jim.

Now, there were two possessions that Jim and Della owned with pride. One was Jim's gold watch that had been his father's and his grandfather's. The other was Della's beautiful hair that fell about her like a cascade of brown waters. It reached below her knee like a garment.

Della nervously and quickly put her hair up, trying to hold back the tears. She put on her old, brown jacket and old, brown hat and fluttered out the door and down the stairs to the street.

She noticed a sign that read: "Mme. Sofronie. Hair Goods of All Kinds." She promptly entered the store and sold her hair for twenty dollars.

With money in hand, she ransacked the stores for Jim's present—a platinum fob chain, simple and chaste in design. It was worthy of Jim's watch and worth the twenty-one dollars.

When Della reached home, she got out her curling irons and covered her head with tiny, close-lying curls.

It was seven o'clock, and Jim was never late. As she waited, she whispered, "Please God, make him think I'm still pretty." Jim closed the door behind him, his eyes fixed upon Della. She could not read his expression, and it terrified her.

"Darling," she cried, "don't look at me that way. I cut off and sold my hair because I couldn't live through Christmas without giving you a beautiful present."

"You've cut off your hair?" asked Jim.

"Don't you like me just as well?" said Della.

He enfolded his Della, then drew a package from his pocket.

"Nothing could make me like my girl any less," he said. "Unwrap that package to see why you had me going at first."

Della tore at the string and paper; there was an ecstatic scream of joy followed by hysterical tears and wails. There lay The Combs—the set of combs that Della had worshipped in a Broadway window. Beautiful combs, pure tortoise shell, with jeweled rims—just the shade to wear in the beautiful, vanished hair.

But she hugged them to her bosom, smiled, and said, "My hair grows so fast, Jim!"

Eagerly, she held the chain out to him upon her open palm.

"Isn't it beautiful, Jim?" she beamed. "I searched all over for it. Give me your watch. I want to see how it looks on it."

Instead of obeying, Jim tumbled down on the couch, put his hands under the back of his head, and smiled.

"Dell," he said, "let's put our Christmas presents away because I sold the watch to get the money to buy your combs."

The magi, as you know, were wonderfully wise men who brought gifts to the Babe in the manger. They invented the art of giving Christmas presents. Being wise, their gifts were no doubt wise ones, possibly bearing the privilege of exchange in case of duplication. And here I have lamely related to you the uneventful chronicle of two foolish children who most unwisely sacrificed for each other the greatest treasures of their house. Let it be said that of all who give gifts, these two were the wisest. They are the magi.

Today, we are going to seek Jesus in prayer. Make these prayers personal to you today using some of the language in today's devotional. Speak directly with God about your heart.

Meet me in _____

_____

_____

Encourage me by _____

_____

_____

Challenge me to _____

_____

_____

Make me more like You in _____

_____

_____

Refresh me by _____

_____

_____

Direct me in _____

_____

_____

Focus me on _____

_____

_____

O holy night! The stars are brightly shining,
It is the night of our dear Savior's birth.
Long lay the world in sin and error pining,
'Til He appear'd and the soul felt its worth.
A thrill of hope the weary world rejoices,
For yonder breaks a new and glorious morn.
Fall on your knees! O hear the angel voices!
O night divine, O night when Christ was born;
O night divine, O night, O night divine.

—FROM "O HOLY NIGHT"
BY JOHN SULLIVAN DWIGHT

Change

Do you, like me, get frustrated when you get stuck in a rut? When you can't seem to escape the monotony of a certain part of life? There are moments when change is so welcomed. Maybe a change of seasons brings renewed appreciation for the beauty in nature. Or a change of a home brings a fresh start to your life. A change in careers can sometimes bring financial freedom or new opportunities. I personally love interacting with my kids as they grow older; it's a change, but it is sweet! Change has the potential to be a beautiful opportunity in the midst of monotony. Sometimes, however, change is less welcome.

I wonder what changes you might be facing this Christmas. Maybe you are celebrating Christmas alone or without a beloved family member this year. Or maybe you're hosting Christmas for the first time and feel overwhelmed. Perhaps you are trying to figure out how to make Christmas special despite fewer presents showing up under the tree. Christmas is full of tradition, but as time goes on, it can also mark seasons of change.

We are not promised a life without change. Change is a part of life that can be expected, but still, we're never quite ready to weather the changes well. In these moments, we must turn to our never-changing, ever-steadfast Jesus, the only unchanging and constant presence in our life. It's in the character and presence of our Savior that we find hope and steadiness in the middle of life's storms. The author of Hebrews reminds us: "Jesus Christ is the same yesterday, today, and forever" (HEBREWS 13:8 NKJV).

This brings me so much comfort. When I think of my own life in the past, present, and future, I can't help but see the different ways God has stepped into my circumstances in different seasons. I have new opportunities to enjoy God now that were less available when I was surrounded by small kids. When I was in the thick of raising babies, there was a dependence on Jesus that I have to work harder to discover now. Change brings about new opportunities to experience the deep and steadfast love of Jesus in your life.

So as you approach Christmas Day, think about how God could meet you in the middle of your changes. Surely there are moments, traditions, people who will show up differently this year than ever before. Rather than being fixated on what's different, how can you look for what is uniquely good about this holiday? What opportunities might you have to look outside your own circumstances and bring about good in the life of another person? Because our joy and our hope come from an unchanging, eternal God, we have the opportunity to find goodness no matter what change we experience!

Today, remind yourself of the goodness of God that you have access to. The satisfaction, contentment, and joy of life with Christ is available because of what He did on the cross for us. No circumstance can alter that truth. How can you remind yourself of God's faithfulness today? Take time to think back on your life and the many changes you have weathered. Do you see God's fingerprints all throughout your life? Do you see the way He made good out of bad and brought hope when you despaired? This is the work of God in your life! As you approach another Christmas, rest in the knowledge that our joy is found in a God who is the same, unchanging, yesterday, today, and forever.

The Christmas Spruce Tree

by *Anna Von Rydingsvärd*

(A NORWEGIAN LEGEND)

Among the tall trees in the forest grew a little spruce tree. It was no taller than a man, and that is very short for a tree. The other trees near it grew so tall and had such large branches that the poor little tree could not grow at all. She liked to listen when the other trees were talking, but it often made her sad.

"I am king of the forest," said the oak. "Look at my huge trunk and my branches. How they reach up toward heaven! I furnish planks for men from which they build their ships. Then I defy the storm on the ocean as I do the thunder in the forest."

"And I go with you over the foaming waves," said the tall straight pine. "I hold up the flapping sails when the ships fly over the ocean."

"And we warm the houses when winter comes and the cold north wind drives the snow before him," said the birches.

"We have the same work to do," said a tall fir tree, and she bowed gracefully, drooping her branches toward the ground.

The little spruce tree could not think of any way in which she could be useful. She decided to ask the other trees in the forest. So she asked the oak, the pine, and the fir, but they were so proud and stately they did not even hear her.

Then she asked the beautiful white birch that stood nearby. "You have no work to do," said the birch, "because you can never grow large enough. Perhaps you might be a Christmas tree, but that is all."

"What is a Christmas tree?" asked the little spruce.

"I do not know exactly," replied the birch. "Sometimes when the days are short and cold and the ground is covered with snow, men come out here into the forest. They look at all the little spruce trees and choose the prettiest, saying, 'This will do for a Christmas tree.' Then they chop it down and carry it away. What they do with it I cannot tell."

The little spruce asked the rabbit that hopped over the snow, and the owls that slept in the pines, and the squirrels that came to find nuts and acorns. But no one knew more than the birch tree. No one could tell what men did with the Christmas trees.

At last a boy came into the forest with an ax in his hand. He looked the little tree all over. "Perhaps this will do for a Christmas tree," he said. So he chopped her down, laid her on a sled, and dragged her home.

The next day the boy sold the tree, and she was taken into a large room and dressed up with popcorn and gilded nuts and candles. Packages of all sizes and shapes, and tiny bags filled with candy, were tied on her branches.

The tree was trembling with the excitement, but she stood as still as she could. "What if I should drop some of this fruit," she thought.

When it began to grow dark, everyone left the room and the tree was alone. She began to feel lonely and to think sad thoughts.

Soon the door opened and a lady came in. She lighted all the candles. How light and glowing it was then! The tree had never even dreamed of anything so beautiful!

Then the children came and danced about the tree, singing a Christmas song. The father played on his violin, and the baby sat in her mother's arms, smiling and cooing.

"Now I know what I was made for," thought the spruce tree. "I was intended to give joy to the little ones, because I, myself, am so small and humble."

Think about at least three qualities of God that have stuck out to you throughout your life.

WRITE IN THE COLUMNS ABOUT HOW EACH QUALITY
SHOWED UP IN THE PAST, IN THE PRESENT, AND HOW
YOU HOPE IT WILL SHOW UP IN THE FUTURE.

QUALITY OF GOD	PAST	PRESENT	FUTURE
PATIENT			
KIND			
GENEROUS			
FORGIVING			
WISE			
POWERFUL			

While shepherds watched
Their flocks by night
All seated on the ground,
The angel of the Lord came down
And glory shone around
And glory shone around.
"Fear not," he said,
For mighty dread
Had seized their troubled minds.
"Glad tidings of great joy I bring
To you and all mankind,
To you and all mankind."

—FROM "WHILE SHEPHERDS
WATCHED THEIR FLOCKS"
BY NAHUM TATE

Refuge

The Christmas season always makes me consider the different people who played a role in the story of Jesus' birth. So many people risked their lives and put their own safety on the line to experience this incredible miracle. Mary traveled while extremely pregnant. She amazes me. And even more amazing—she gave birth in a *stable*. The wise men risked their lives when they misled King Herod. The shepherds left their fields, putting their livelihood on the line. But all these people willingly sacrificed and risked their own safety because of the promise of God's goodness and presence in their lives.

We rarely experience that sort of danger, and yet it is still so difficult for us to rely on the Lord in times of trouble. I often find myself leaning more on the comforts in my own life, the "wisdom" of people (and what I can discover online), or the protections of my home to make me feel safe. I wonder sometimes what comfort and security I might be missing out on because I rely more on my own strength than the strength of the Lord. If I put myself in the shoes of Mary or the wise men, I wonder if I'd have the strength to do what they did. When I consider the many stories of incredible and ordinary people in the Bible who risked their lives for the sake of another or the sake of the Gospel, I'm challenged to think about where my help comes from.

The authors of the book of Psalms often call out to God in times of trouble. I love the way Psalm 46 captures this: "God is our refuge and strength, a very present help in trouble. Therefore we will not fear, even though the earth be removed, and though the mountains be carried into the midst of the sea; though its waters roar and be troubled, though the mountains shake with its swelling" (VERSES 1-3 NKJV).

Do you ever feel like the earth is giving way? Like the mountains might fall into the sea? Like the waters are roaring and the mountains are shaking? There are moments in life when I certainly feel this way. We're often surrounded by chaos. The world isn't always a happy place. People can be SO unkind. It's so easy to choose fear in the moments when we feel like everything around us is falling apart. It's natural to look around at difficult circumstances and things that feel out of control and conclude that we are alone and sinking.

But these words give us comfort in the midst of great troubles: "God is our refuge and strength." God is our refuge, our safe space, the place where we can finally relax and feel at home. He is the place where we can lay our heads in rest despite the world feeling chaotic and out of control. He is our strength. He gives us the ability to keep going when we feel empty. He sustains us in seasons when we really feel like we have nothing left to give.

What situations in your life feel too overwhelming to step into? Are there relationships that feel too risky? Conversations that feel like too much? Obstacles that feel too daunting to overcome? Take comfort in these words: God is "a very present help in trouble."

Do you feel the ever-present help of your God? Does His presence allow you to risk your own safety and security for the sake of what He is calling you to? Think this Christmas season of Mary, the wise men, and the shepherds. Can you follow in their footsteps and risk what you hold most precious for the sake of being in the presence of Jesus? God is with you and will give you strength!

The Christmas Story

Luke 2:1–20 (CSB)

In those days a decree went out from Caesar Augustus that the whole empire should be registered. This first registration took place while Quirinius was governing Syria. So everyone went to be registered, each to his own town.

Joseph also went up from the town of Nazareth in Galilee, to Judea, to the city of David, which is called Bethlehem, because he was of the house and family line of David, to be registered along with Mary, who was engaged to him and was pregnant. While they were there, the time came for her to give birth. Then she gave birth to her firstborn son, and she wrapped him tightly in cloth and laid him in a manger, because there was no guest room available for them.

In the same region, shepherds were staying out in the fields and keeping watch at night over their flock. Then an angel of the Lord stood before them, and the glory of the Lord shone around them, and they were terrified. But the angel said to them, "Don't be afraid, for look, I proclaim to you good news of great joy that will be for all the people: Today in the city of David a Savior was born for you, who is the Messiah, the Lord. This will be the sign for you: You will find a baby wrapped tightly in cloth and lying in a manger."

Suddenly there was a multitude of the heavenly host with the angel, praising God and saying:

Glory to God in the highest heaven,
and peace on earth to people He favors!

When the angels had left them and returned to heaven, the shepherds said to one another, "Let's go straight to Bethlehem and see what has happened, which the Lord has made known to us."

They hurried off and found both Mary and Joseph, and the baby who was lying in the manger. After seeing them, they reported the message they were told about this child, and all who heard it were amazed at what the shepherds said to them. But Mary was treasuring up all these things in her heart and meditating on them. The shepherds returned, glorifying and praising God for all the things they had seen and heard, which were just as they had been told.

There's a common phrase that says "Let go, and let God." Today spend time thinking about what areas of your life you might need to let go of to let God work in you and to fill you with joy this Christmas season.

Letting Go

WHAT ARE YOU HOLDING ON TO
IN LIFE THAT YOU NEED
TO RELEASE CONTROL OVER?

Example: I want to let go of resentment toward a friend.

I want to let go of _____

_____

_____

_____

I want to let go of _____

_____

_____

_____

I want to let go of _____

_____

_____

_____

Let God

WHAT DO YOU WANT TO
LET GOD DO IN YOUR LIFE?

Example: I want to let God fill me with contentment.

I want to let God _____

_____

_____

_____

I want to let God _____

_____

_____

_____

I want to let God _____

_____

_____

_____

Which areas of your life do you think you need to release control of so you can have more joy? *(Check all that apply.)*

☐ Relationships

☐ Physical comfort

☐ Scheduling

☐ Family

☐ Health

☐ Money

☐ Food

Explain how letting God take control of these areas and taking refuge in His ability instead of your own would change your circumstances:

_____

_____

_____

_____

_____

_____

_____

_____

Write a brief prayer asking God to take control, change your attitude toward your circumstances, and give you joy this Christmas season:

_____

_____

_____

_____

_____

_____

_____

_____

_____

Joy in Sacrifice

I love the moments in the Christmas story that describe the arrival of the wise men. Imagine their journey. They left from a faraway place in the east in pursuit of the King. Herod sent them to Bethlehem to find this new King, and when they found Him, "they were overjoyed. . . . They bowed down and worshiped Him" (MATTHEW 2:10-11 NIV). They showered the newborn King with gifts of gold, frankincense, and myrrh.

Because the Christmas story is so familiar, I think the impact of the wise men's journey is often lost on us. We lose sight of the time and resources these faithful men poured into their journey and focus instead on the unique gifts they bring to Jesus.

When we stop to think about the role these wise men from the east played in the Christmas story, I think we find that we have the opportunity to live like these men. We are far more similar to them than we might first realize, and we have far more to learn from them than we could imagine. Their story is one that is marked by sacrifice and relentless pursuit of their King. These men gave up years of their lives to find the boy King. They sacrificed precious resources to bring gifts to a toddler who surely couldn't appreciate the value of their gifts. They risked their lives by not returning to Herod to report on Jesus' whereabouts. They were obedient in all these things simply because of what was foretold in the Old Testament and dreams from an angel. They were not promised any reward or special treatment for living in such a radical way.

In a season that often revolves around getting rather than giving and comfort over sacrifice, it's so important to stop and consider what we might need to learn from the wise men. As you approach Christmas this year, what might you need to sacrifice? Are there areas of your life that need to be set aside to take care of what God has placed in front of you? Is there a work project that is stealing your joy and attention from your family? Are there items on your Christmas wish list that are keeping you from enjoying simple moments around a fireplace with loved ones? Is there something standing in your way of pursuing Jesus instead of comfort and temporary happiness?

The moment in the wise men's story that sticks out the most to me is when they arrived and met Jesus. The Bible says they were *overjoyed*. So often we miss the reality that a life marked by following and chasing after Jesus will not lead to being underwhelmed, dissatisfied, or living a life of deprivation. The wise men didn't show up after years of sacrificing their time, their bodies, and their resources only to find Jesus and receive a pat on the back for their obedience. They experienced JOY! It's the joy that only meeting Jesus can elicit. It's a joy that causes grown men to fall at the feet of a baby and give their precious goods. A joy that causes these men to risk their lives to protect their young King's life.

Have you known this joy? Have you felt this deep satisfaction? If you haven't, perhaps consider what stands in your way. Are you chasing after something other than Jesus? Hoping that you'll find that incredible fulfillment in a promotion? A spouse? A new wardrobe? A better exercise routine? Dear friends, nothing, truly *nothing*, will satisfy you other than standing in Jesus' presence. Take a page from the wise men's book: drop everything for the incredible joy that comes from finding Jesus.

The Wise Men from the East

Matthew 2:1–12 (NLT)

Jesus was born in Bethlehem in Judea, during the reign of King Herod. About that time some wise men from eastern lands arrived in Jerusalem, asking, "Where is the newborn king of the Jews? We saw His star as it rose, and we have come to worship Him."

King Herod was deeply disturbed when he heard this, as was everyone in Jerusalem. He called a meeting of the leading priests and teachers of religious law and asked, "Where is the Messiah supposed to be born?"

"In Bethlehem in Judea," they said, "for this is what the prophet wrote:

'And you, O Bethlehem in the land of Judah,
    are not least among the ruling cities of Judah,
for a ruler will come from you
    who will be the shepherd for my people Israel.'"

Then Herod called for a private meeting with the wise men, and he learned from them the time when the star first appeared. Then he told them, "Go to Bethlehem and search carefully for the child. And when you find Him, come back and tell me so that I can go and worship Him, too!"

After this interview the wise men went their way. And the star they had seen in the east guided them to Bethlehem. It went ahead of them and stopped over the place where the child was. When they saw the star, they were filled with joy! They entered the house and saw the child with His mother, Mary, and they bowed down and worshiped Him. Then they opened their treasure chests and gave Him gifts of gold, frankincense, and myrrh.

When it was time to leave, they returned to their own country by another route, for God had warned them in a dream not to return to Herod.

Today, let's have a brainstorm session. Think about things in your life that get in the way of experiencing true joy in Jesus. In the thought bubbles provided, try to just begin the thinking process about what you might need to sacrifice or make space for in order to be "overjoyed" by Jesus. Don't feel the pressure of making any huge commitments, but make space for God to move in your heart while you think over these things.

We three kings of Orient are,
Bearing gifts we traverse afar,
Field and fountain,
Moor and mountain,
Following yonder star.
O star of wonder, star of night,
Star with royal beauty bright,
Westward leading.
Still proceeding,
Guide us to thy perfect light.

—FROM "WE THREE KINGS
BY J. H. HOPKINS JR.

Want more from Candace?
You can find her *One Step Closer Bible*,
along with her series of Devotional
Guides and inspirational gifts on
dayspring.com as well as several
retail stores near you.

About the Author

CANDACE CAMERON BURE is an actress, producer, and *New York Times* bestselling author. Beloved by millions worldwide for her roles as D.J. Tanner in the iconic family sitcoms *Full House* and *Fuller House*, in Hallmark Channel movies, as former cohost of *The View*, and as a *Dancing with the Stars* season 18 finalist, Candace is both outspoken and passionate about her family and faith. She and her husband, Val, have been married for 25 years. They have three grown children and live with their much-loved dog, Boris, in the L.A. area.

Dear Friend,

This book was prayerfully crafted with you, the reader, in mind. Every word, every sentence, every page was thoughtfully written, designed, and packaged to encourage you—right where you are this very moment. At DaySpring, our vision is to see every person experience the life-changing message of God's love. So, as we worked through rough drafts, design changes, edits, and details, we prayed for you to deeply experience His unfailing love, indescribable peace, and pure joy. It is our sincere hope that through these Truth-filled pages your heart will be blessed, knowing that God cares about you—your desires and disappointments, your challenges and dreams.

He knows. He cares. He loves you unconditionally.

BLESSINGS!
THE DAYSPRING BOOK TEAM